MAKING
KINDNESS
THE NORM,

Building a Block of Civility

Prof. *Shakuntala Reddy*, (Rose) Ph.D

Foreword by
HRH DR. CLYDE RIVERS
President of iChange Nations USA

Printed in the United States of America

YPN Publishing & Media

MISSION STATEMENT

We have Kingdom Integrated Notions for Developing the Nation into Endeavouring Solicitous and Sympathetic citizens

VISION

We are dedicated to bringing humanity back to its God given purpose of living a fulfilled and accepted life of civility by leaving a trail of KINDNESS wherever we go.

DEDICATION

A very special thank you to Vee, my dear husband, of 35 years. He has been my rock of Gibraltar, who had spoiled me rotten. My children and I are proud to call him Pa. His undeniable dedication in terms of time, patience, tolerance, support, vocabulary and being the idea guy has been prodigious. Glaucoma has been the thief of his sight, making him unable to see the beauty of his contribution, nonetheless, he continues to extend his ideas incorporated into my writing. Thank you, Pa.

Trevishka, the editor of all my written work, thank you for your eye for errors and the corrective text provided.

You are the best and worst critic, who is ready to engage in positive criticism; with a fight. I see myself in you every day and am glad for your growth and adventure, not only outdoors but in and through your academic prowess.

Renesska, my talented, creative genius who still has much growing up to do, thank you for your tech-savvy mind, which I sometimes underestimate. Continue to love and serve everyone you connect with.

Yashika, the daughter of another mother, you are truly one of my girls. Thank you for your tolerance and for being my sounding board for bouncing off ideas. Your patience in teaching me social media stuff is highly valued. Thank you for looking up to Pa, the girls and me as your extended family. You have accepted all our quirkiness and added yours to it.

His Royal Highness **Professor Clyde Rivers, Prof. Michal Pitzl** and the United Graduate College and Seminary International (UGCSI) Team for their mentorship and guidance. This book is the brainchild of the Searcherdemics and the Authorship programme, in which I participated in. Thank you for believing in me.

 Heavenly Father, without You this would not have become a reality. Lord, You spoke the word through Your handmaiden Pastor Shirley Munsami, who awakened the dormant desire to become an author. This is the fruit of my labour of love of Your kingdom, which is ready to impact and transform lives bringing glory to your name. Lord, Your word have I hid in my heart, that I can do ALL things because You give me the strength, Philippians 4:13.

ACKNOWLEDGEMENTS

Nothing comes together without a great and talented team of people who makes things happen. Vee, thank you for allowing me to keep on writing without expecting me to go to bed when you couldn't wait any longer. You were always keen to listen to my ideas and provide your ideologies.

Trevishka, my literary agent and editor; despite your ultra-busyness have always made time to proofread my efforts with positive criticism, which hasn't always been easily digested.

Joey Breukelman, my dear old friend, had been my editor

who proofread this manuscript, thank you.

Thank you to YPN Publishing & Media who has printed these hard copies and eBooks.

FOREWORD

Dr Rose Reddy is a true pioneer voice of kindness for the entire world. This amazing woman is truly a class writer by herself. I have personally worked around the world in over 60 nations and Dr Rose Reddy, is truly a trailblazer of Kindness with Civility in action. She has created programs to teach children kindness and respect for each other at a young age. I call her a prophet of Kindness, she has a vision for a world with Kindness and Civility and she has implemented programs at her school to magnify kindness and the young generation is pursuing the narrative because of one lady. We now understand why this amazing lady was one of the African Civility Educators of the year for 2021 because of the work she has done in her school while engaging the community of Richard's Bay, South Africa. Her name will go down in history as a true pioneer of kindness for the whole world to see.

Prof. Rose is a unique one-of-a-kind thinker. I promise you as you read this book you will receive an impartation of a new way of viewing things. Learning the "how-to" is so necessary in the world we live in today.

The great innovators create what you want and leave an imprint that outlives them. This book is a new paradigm of thinking. I encourage everyone to open their heart and move to think differently because their imprint is created to be eternal. The privilege of reading this book created by Prof. Rose will impact your life in the world.

She uses Civility to unlock the power and potential of humanity's greatest asset: kindness.

Let's build a kinder world together.

HRH Dr Clyde Rivers
World Civility Leader
President and Founder of I Change Nations the USA

CONTENTS

Let us all speak
KIND WORDS
to each other
_____
in person. to others. online.

"Kindness is always Fashionable,
and always welcome."
–Amelia Barr

THE INTROSPECTION

This book is a revelation of what God had locked inside of us. Through introspection and much exploration into our hearts and minds, we can find strategies to be the change that we want others to see in us. Then we will be able to connect with them and extract the hidden talents and potentials that are buried under grief, sorrow, fear, abuse, neglect and low self-esteem. The paradigm of the world system of selfishness will be converted to selflessness. The fabric of society will become a patchwork of differences with the fruit of the spirit being the underlying conversion and binding agent. Hardened hearts of stone will be melted into hearts of flesh, with love, compassion and mercy. God, the author and finisher of our being, will alter our spiritual make-up and modify us to run with the new vision set before us which will enable us to accomplish the following:

- Humanity to learn and experience the solutions to societal problems.

- Each individual responds and reacts uniquely, providing alternate Biblical solutions.

- Respond to and create new and different solutions for the same challenges.

- Change their movements and actions to practical ones, not preached ones.

- Become forerunners and pioneers in new, uncharted and undiscovered fields.

- Arouse all the hidden talents buried under grief, rejection and denial.

- Find new information, strategies and learning systems and introduce them to the world.

- Become entrepreneurs and searchers not researchers.

The Coronavirus pandemic of the year 2020 had wreaked havoc in our lives, homes, schools, workplace, businesses and economy. As Searchers, we did not sit back and grumble about our circumstances, but we became proactive and met the needs of our family, friends and the needy. We complied with all the protocol measures that were implemented and made the most with what we had available, like the Virtuous Women of Proverbs 31. We cooked, baked, sewed, looked after family, and friends and worked with our hands. We comforted those who were terrified and depressed, by making them see the Light of the World shining over and protecting them. We removed every shred of darkness that was hovering over them through the Word of God, which gave them hope.

We adopted the new terminology and phrases such as social distancing, sanitisation and wearing of masks to ensure that we did not contract the coronavirus. Masks, which became part of our daily attire, had to be made or purchased. COVID-19 had stirred up the creative genii inside most of us. We embarked on making the most creative masks for ourselves and donated to the less fortunate. New ways of thinking had created the most unusual meals to feed the family, who were afraid of frequenting the shopping malls as we had done before. We baked bread, and made rotis, (Indian bread) naans, bread buns and rolls. We made homemade cheese(paneer), pies, cakes and packed them away in freezers for later use. Our hidden culinary skills were stretched to their limits, producing unprecedented meals. The family was pleased with a wide variety of meals. That created an even stronger bond with each of us. Those life-long learning proficiencies that had lain dormant had been reawakened making families proud and expectant for something new each day.

Learners who had missed out on the regular teaching and learning process, provided by teachers at school, had these alternative methods presented to them.

They were taught remotely, by using online resources, uploaded lessons, video-recorded lessons, Zoom lessons and Google classrooms. Online learning which was the norm for me for the past 15 years, became the new normal. It instilled fear and trepidation about what is to come next for most people. The Y generation who are so technologically savvy thrived on the digital learning methodology. Their results were quite amazing too. An unorthodox relationship and respect between teachers, parents and learners developed. Struggling learners find fun new ways of learning. Other learners were excited to have more media time which was a bonus for them.

For those learners who did not have access to data to participate in the new online schooling system, they had access to lessons made available via television and radio stations at no extra cost. Workbooks were drawn up for parents to collect via a drive-through to keep learners purposefully occupied and up to date on the syllabus. The Searcher was looking inwards for solutions from the Holy Spirit Educator to overcome the challenges actively.

Education became more and more digitized and affordable since the whole education system had been shut down during the lockdown. A very big thank you to technology, because classes had begun again. Online classes which were possible only for adults at tertiary levels had now become accessible to children of all ages.

Tertiary Institutions were now saving on infrastructural costs, making studies more affordable and accessible to students who face challenges being full-time day students. The online education system is increasing; making every sector of society more accessible to education from the comfort and security of their homes. New and innovative methods were and are used to facilitate teaching and learning.

Churches were closed to prevent the spread of the virus, making families gather together to have services at home. There were more people praying then than ever before. Online sermons were broadcast, creating a widespread listenership, making it easily common place to the general public who do not go to church. That was a global deposition of the Gospel, which brought hope in a time of fear and consternation. There was a greater awareness of and search for God than ever before.

The greatest positive that arose from this pandemic was the reuniting of families who had an opportunity to bond again and develop better and stronger relationships with each other. Work was no longer an excuse for the lack of family time. Parents worked remotely from home, with the advantage of being with their families to meet both physical and emotional needs. Neglected children benefited by spending more time with their parents, having regular mealtimes and being helped with schoolwork. All the extra parental attention at home had produced positive relational benefits and great academic results.

Parents got to keep a watchful eye on their older children and their whereabouts, which resulted in a reduction in crime and unsolicited behaviour. Personal visitation being prohibited caused family members to reconnect with loved ones virtually and more frequently.

Innovative measures such as texting, video calling, zoom meetings, and team meetings had been invented to remain connected with each other. Products and different service delivery methods had been created to attract and sustain contacts with colleagues, customers, employees and loved ones. There has been a new wave of online tools and software which has helped us to shift effortlessly into digital classrooms and virtual office spaces. It has opened doors to online interviews with as many as fifty or more people simultaneously. It helped to identify and enhance the workflow and processes that are crucial for the smooth running of organisations. Self-diagnosed bots have paved the way to touchless biometric attendance systems. Health questionnaires are filled in virtually to allow employees and learners access to schools and workplaces. Our school had a "COVID-19 PASSPORT,"

Richards Bay Primary School
Screening Questionnaire

Name: .... Gr............Signature:......................

DATE	Temperature		Cough		Loss of smell or taste		Body aches		Shortness of breath		Nausea, vomiting, diarrhoea		Been to a doctor for COVID-19	
	H	L	Y	N	Y	N	Y	N	Y	N	Y	N	Y	N

DO NOT REPORT TO SCHOOL IF:
1. Showing any of these symptoms.

2. Any family member residing in the same home is tested positive for COVID-19.
3. Any family member is in isolation for COVID-19.

(health questionnaire) that allowed learners entry into the school building.

Better hygiene practice became a lifestyle to preserve our posterity. Frequent disinfection, handwashing and sanitisation had become the norm to keep the virus away. Not touching MEN, Mouth, Eyes and the Nose was the rule of thumb, because those areas were more prone to receive infection. Remembering to cough and sneeze in the crook of one's elbow if no tissues or handkerchiefs were available was the next safety measure implemented. Shaking of hands and hugging in greeting was prohibited; instead fist bumps, elbow tipping and foot thumping was the acceptable form of greeting. The traditional Indian "Namaste "had become commonplace, signifying that although we were physically apart, we were still socially connected.

With reduced economic activity, street crimes such as assault, stealing, breaking into homes and vehicles and road accidents were reduced. Unfortunately, domestic violence was on the rise; because victims were housebound with perpetrators and had no way of escape.

Businesses being run remotely had helped to reduce costs in terms of rental of business space, where large physical space was no longer necessary. Remote working became mainstream. Distance and travelling was no longer a challenge. It reduces exhaust emissions and fuel prices.

From an environmental perspective skies were bluer, dolphins were swimming closer to the shoreline, with reduced fishing and ocean activities. There was a reduction in pollution, yielding significant health benefits. Other infectious diseases were fading from hospital emergency rooms.

The COVID pandemic had presented us with challenges, which by the grace of God we were able to overcome. Countries around the world are still fighting this scourge, but we are in a race of survivors who will not be defeated. It has been a long and grief-stricken ordeal, but with our positive attitude we see victory.

WHAT IS KINDNESS?

Aristotle defined kindness as, "Helpfulness towards someone in need, not in return for anything, nor for the advantage of the helper himself, but for that of the person helped."

Michael Card's definition raised the bar higher when he said, "Kindness is when the person from whom I have the right to expect nothing, gives me everything."

Who better we offer the paramount gratitude to? Than to our Lord and Saviour Jesus Christ, who gave His life so that we will not be condemned to eternal damnation, but through His sacrifice, we would be saved. God demonstrates the ultimate technique of kindness through the gospel, by giving us the ultimate gift of unconditional love. We have been saved through God's kindness and have been adopted into His family as children of the Most-High God.

We are hereby called to imitate His kindness towards people around us. Colossians 3:12, commands us to, "Put on bowels of mercies, kindness, humbleness of mind, meekness, longsuffering; forbearing one another and forgiving one another."

Above all, we are called to put on charity, which is the bond of perfection. Charity is kindness, tolerance, humanity, compassion, generosity, altruism, goodwill, benevolence, sympathy, understanding and consideration. When displaying any of the above we are extending the arm of kindness.

Just as a rose called by any other name will still smell as sweet. Kindness called by any of the above names has the same desired outcome.

Altruism is the unselfish concern for other people by doing things simply out of a desire to help, not out of obligation, duty, loyalty or religion. It is not an act of reciprocity. It is simple acts like giving alms to a beggar, holding the door for others to enter, jumping in to save a drowning child, replacing a punctured tyre, giving first aid to an injured person, and being an organ and blood donor. Sharing your resources, despite the personal costs as long as it benefits anyone, not only family and friends. It is prosocial behaviour that is motivated by internalized values and morals. Our interactions and relationships with others have a major influence on altruistic behaviour and a significant impact on others around us. Studies have shown that children who observed acts of altruism were more likely to exhibit altruistic actions. Children do as you do, not as you say.

Altruistic behaviour has proven to also be beneficial to the benefactor subliminally; better mental and physical well-being. Lower mortality rates, increased happiness and healthy lifestyles were the results. We inspire others to do likewise, not to separate ourselves from the needy, but to practice empathy.

Benevolence; is an inclination to be kind, by helping the old cross the street, carrying the shopping for the aged, tutoring the academically challenged without charging tuition fees. It is basically the desire to be nice and do good deeds. History records examples of kind gestures that changed history.

Compassion is being moved by the suffering of others and motivated to alleviate that suffering. Qualities of compassion are kindness and perseverance; patience and wisdom; warmth and resolve. It prompts people to go out of their way to help relieve the physical, mental and emotional pains of others. Kind and compassionate people are more satisfied with their lives, have stronger relationships and have better physical and mental health. Vulnerable people who have kindness and compassion shown to them feel good and worthwhile. It increases their well-being, overcomes loneliness, improves self-esteem and builds healthy relationships. Acts of compassion have reciprocal actions; recipients are generally kind and generous to others too. People have a tendency to pay it forward, volunteer or make donations in return for what they have received.

Humanity is defined as the quality of being humane. Humane is marked by compassion, sympathy and consideration for humans or animals. It never hurts to treat people with kindness, whether it's with loved ones or strangers. "For every child, a fair chance. For every child, it is an act of humanity." UNICEF. They created this funding to provide emergency food and healthcare to children and mothers in countries devastated by war. Their philosophy is that children are entitled to respect, care and support. A single act of humanity, big or small, can go a long way towards helping a refugee or migrant child who has arrived in an unfamiliar place cold, hungry and afraid. Providing these essential services with a welcoming smile, a helping hand and emotional support as rites of passage as children mature is a key to ensuring the well-being of children during this transition. Children's lives are saved, their rights are defended and they are helped to fulfil their potential.

1.   A letter that saves Jane Austen

In 1783, Jane Austen and her sister Cassandra became very ill with diphtheria- a potential sore throat. Mr

Cawley, the teacher made no attempt to notify the parents, but Jane Cooper, the cousin took it upon herself to write to her aunt informing her that Jane's life was in danger. On receipt of the letter her mother took a herbal remedy and went to rescue the girls. The sisters recovered under their mother's care. Without her cousin's intervention, Jane Austen would have died depriving the world of her outstanding talent as a novelist.

2.   Elizabeth Fry's visit to Newgate Gaol, (1780-1845)

Elizabeth Fry was a British social reformer who was commemorated on the UK's £5 note, for her most philanthropic project: reform of the female side of Newgate Gaol. She was a mother of eleven children, a social activist, and a Quaker minister. By the early 19th century she turned her attention to the plight of the poor, by distributing aid and founding a Sunday School for children. She later established a school for poor girls and organised a smallpox vaccination programme for the children in the surrounding villages. In 1813 she visited the Newgate Gaol to distribute clothing to the female prisoners. She was appalled at the living conditions and the sight of two women taking the clothes of a dead baby to dress a living one. By 1816, not much had changed, propelling her to organise a school for the children with a matron to watch over the prisoners. She found useful work, such as knitting and sewing for the women. She also formed the Ladies' Newgate Association, the members would visit the prison daily to supervise the matron, give religious instruction and mentor the prisoners. New rules were introduced, forbidding swearing, quarrelling, immoral conversation and improper books. The voluntary submission of the prisoners with Elizabeth won the support of the gaol and the city authorities. The Elizabeth Fry Refuge was a foundation that won public recognition for the release of female prisoners in 1849.

ELIZABETH FRY
1780–1845

3.   The hiding of Anne Franks' family

During the reign of Adolf Hitler and the Nazi party in 1933, Otto and Edith Frank and their daughters escaped to the Netherlands from Germany. They hid in Miep Gies' annex above his office in Amsterdam on 6 July 1942. They helped hide a number of people for the next two years. During the two years, Miep Gies and other helpers showed kindness by bringing food, supplies and news from outside. The friendship and kindness shown by her was a lifeline for Anne, who kept a diary about her experiences and thoughts while in hiding. On 4 August 1944 everyone in the annex was arrested. Anne and her sister Margot were sent to a concentration camp in Germany, where the girls later died of typhus. After the arrest, Miep Gies found the diary and gave it to Anne's dad in 1945, who was the only survivor of the war. Anne Frank's diary was published in the Netherlands on 25 June 1947. It is one of the most famous and bestselling books of all time.

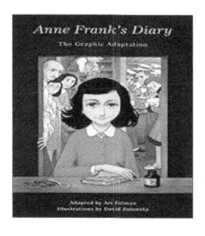

Proverbs 21:21, He who pursues righteousness and kindness finds life, prosperity and honour. CJB

There is a promise of prosperity and honour for those who are good, virtuous and kind. Every act of kindness never goes unnoticed and will be paid back in full in due season.

Romans 2:4, Do you have contempt for God, who is very kind to you, puts up with you, and deals patiently with you? Don't you realize that it is God's kindness that is trying to lead you to Him and change the way you think and act? GW

Let us be tolerant of the less perfect, unkind people around us. We are not perfect, but we should strive every day to do that which is pleasing in the sight of God. God is patient with us, let us try to emulate Him and embrace our counterparts, by being patient and kind to them.

1 Corinthians 1:4, I never stop thanking my God for being kind enough to give us Christ Jesus, who helps us speak and understand so well. CEV.

We are taught through God's word to be kind, understanding and repentant and to lead others to do the same in no better way than by example.

Who makes us feel good to be with? The people we feel good to be with are the ones who are kind. They are the ones who follow through with their promises, who are always ready to help out and who go out of their way to do acts of kindness. When we are with them, we want to treat them the same way we want to be treated.

The way we treat others does matter. If we are judgmental, don't be surprised if we find ourselves being judged. If we gossip, we may find that we are the object of gossip. The reverse is also true. If we are forgiving, we will be forgiven. If we are kind, we will be treated with kindness. It's our choice.

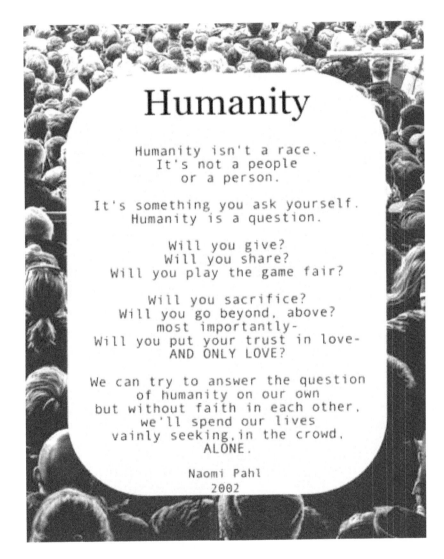

Humanity

Humanity isn't a race.
It's not a people
or a person.

It's something you ask yourself.
Humanity is a question.

Will you give?
Will you share?
Will you play the game fair?

Will you sacrifice?
Will you go beyond, above?
most importantly-
Will you put your trust in love-
AND ONLY LOVE?

We can try to answer the question
of humanity on our own
but without faith in each other,
we'll spend our lives
vainly seeking, in the crowd,
ALONE.

Naomi Pahl
2002

KINDNESS SPRINKLED LIKE CONFETTI

Words resonate in our minds long after they are heard, either through song, speech or from books; therefore, choose what you listen to and read. Those words that you listen to have either a positive impact or a devastating effect on you and future generations. Our thoughts rule our lives, therefore, we have to choose carefully what we ponder. Our thoughts are not harmless or meaningless, they are potent and determine our potentials, abilities, capabilities and disabilities.

According to J. C. Robledo, "In reality, the sum of your thoughts leads to the sum of your actions, which leads to the sum of who you are." Our thoughts lead to our actions and manifest in our facial expressions and speech. When we feel happy, it is expressed in broad smiles, bright eyes, happy laughter and cheery conversations.

Our optimistic attitude is contagious and inadvertently makes others around us happy too. Our thoughts become what we say and what we say and do are imitated by others. Our thoughts become our actions, which model our behaviour. When we think kind thoughts, we speak kind words and end up doing kind deeds. Our actions become reactions in others; love recreates love, and kindness begets kindness. Whatever we think, say and do forms an echo reaction in the world around us. The echo of our thoughts and actions passes through slowly, creating a ripple through the universe. Like social media, it touches lives and sets trends which are followed by like-minded people. We are the echoes of our former generations, we repeat what our parents did and said. Our thoughts, words and actions transcend ourselves, spreading like viruses.

If it is positive, it can propel us forward by edifying and inspiring others. If it is negative, it could drag us down into defeat and depression.

Our thoughts are reflected back to us, if we are kind, we receive kindness back, if we are hateful, we receive hate back. "Remember this: Mind your mind. Mind your thinking. What we think has a way of manifesting itself into reality." J. C. Robledo

Showing kindness to those who expect rejection may be rejected initially because they are suspicious of us. They may feel that we have a hidden agenda, and are taking advantage by flattering them. After a while, when they have built trust and believe in us, the kindness that we show them will be like sprinkling little bits of confetti that flutter around bringing joy, and colour, not only physically, but mentally and spiritually. The sprinkling of kindness, wherever and whenever, will kindle a sparkle of hope, within the heart and there will emerge a gurgling stream of emotion that cannot be hidden but revealed as lopsided smiles, quiet laughter and even hugs. That crooked smile that we receive is just a tenuous reflection of what we've given, through our speech, actions and embrace.

A repetition of that attitude and mannerism will not only open the eyes of expectation, and the hearts of reception; but will have arms extended awaiting an embrace. Every act of kindness will be acknowledged by the less kind. That sense of anticipation will be rewarded, little by little, day by day. What was meant for them will find its way, transforming through transference. Lopsided smiles, quiet laughs and quick hugs will be changed into beaming smiles, cacophonous laughter, big bear hugs and terms of endearments.

Kindness is a fruit of the Holy Spirit, which is borne from being fertilized and nurtured by the Word of God (our Lord Jesus Christ). It is reflected as behaviour or character trait which is marked by acts of generosity, consideration, sympathy and concern for others. These actions should be performed without expecting praise or reward. It is acknowledged as a virtue of honesty, respect, compassion, justice, gratitude, gentleness, humility and courage. Practising kindness will spread around the world as a ripple effect, impacting both the giver and receiver. Kindness is a universal language, which the blind can see and the deaf can hear. Go forth and practice acts of kindness, even randomly; it will make a difference.

A young woman was struggling with overcoming her battle and treatment for cancer, when one day she stepped out and found a painted rock on her porch, with these words emblazoned on it. "The struggle you are experiencing today will be your strength tomorrow." Those kind words gave her courage, peace and hope to confront her struggles with all the side effects of chemotherapy. The kind words that we speak impact the future, without our knowledge. **Let our words be like apples of gold in a silver carving, Proverbs 25:11**

I am a cancer survivor; I owe my accelerated recovery to the kindness shown to me by all the people in my circle of life. The ardent prayers of family and friends, the kind words of encouragement and the nurture and care of my dear beloved husband, loving children, friends and my church family. I remember fondly all the people who sat at my side to alleviate my fears during my chemotherapy and radiation sessions at the Richards Bay Medical Institution. The positive and reassuring advice of my Oncologist, Dr Smitha Abraham eliminated all my fears of cancer and its effects. By the grace of God, I was fortunate not to experience the devastating side effects of that monstrous disease, after receiving eight sessions of chemotherapy and 30 sessions of radiation. I welcomed the desired weight loss.

With very short hair, and no balding, I was able to conquer all the giants of shame, fear and worry, through the word of my testimony, my daily attendance to work at Richards Bay Primary School, and my unwavering diligence to church attendance at New Life Ministries.

I was nominated to be a speaker at a cancer survivor conference, to provide hope and inspiration to other cancer patients.

I attended chemotherapy and radiation after a day at school and returned to work the following day. My duties at work and church continued as normal with no leave of absence. During my treatment I enrolled at Faith Bible College and completed my Advanced Christian Counselling Course, which enabled me to acquire a practice number for counselling. Studying the Word of God kept me focused and enabled me to overcome all the whispers of the enemy that tried to allow doubt and trepidation to set in.

My faith and trust in God for my healing grew in leaps and bounds. This is my testimony of the healing hand of God upon me.

Kindness is infectious, it can spread like wildfire, so light the flame and watch it engulf the nation, consuming doubt, fear, chaos and confusion like a raging inferno. It will remove fear and replace it with confidence and power. Judgment will no longer be clouded, thoughts will not be cluttered and people will no longer be kept guessing, but will have clarity. **For God has not given us a spirit of fear and timidity, but of power, love and self-discipline.** (2 Timothy 1:7).

When we look at a seed, which is a tiny object in comparison to our size, do we see its potential? No, we don't, but inside that seed is a potential to grow into a colossal tree, beautifying its surrounding aesthetically, bearing delicious, sometimes edible fruit and food for us, birds, insects and animals and homes for creatures large and tiny. That one seed produces a harvest of hundreds, if not thousands of other seeds that will reproduce after its genus.

A little sprinkling of kindness will have the same effect; producing a crop, that we may not even get to harvest, but will be pollinated wherever we go. Our influence will shine through the windows of our soul producing a gradual transformation, eventually impacting the universe resulting in the following:

- We will yield victors out of victims.
- Will experience triumph from trouble.
- Will see acceptance from outcasts.
- Will know nice from naughty.
- Will share in the tranquillity from anger.
- Will delight at happiness from sadness.
- Will boast about our excitement from misery.
- Will celebrate with progress from regression.
- Will applaud success from failure.
- Will rejoice with the Lord for the complete transformation from inside out.

Romans 12:2, Don't become like the people of this world. Instead, change the way you think. Then you will always be able to determine what God really wants. That is good, pleasing and perfect, (GW).

We must take our everyday ordinary life; our sleeping, eating, going to work and walking around and place it before God as an offering. He will turn our ordinary existence into extraordinary experiences to impact the lives of others in our circle of influence. We should embrace the fact that what God does for us is the BEST and that we should go forth and exalt Him. We should not become so well adjusted to OUR culture that we fit into it without even thinking, INSTEAD we should fix our attention on God and we will be changed from the INSIDE out. There will be a complete metamorphosis.

Metamorphosis is a biological process by which an animal physically develops after birth or hatching, involving a conspicuous and relatively abrupt change in the animal's body structure through cell growth and differentiation. (Wikipedia)

The definition says that it is a change by natural or supernatural means. It could be earth moving, mind blowing and life changing. Supernaturally, in **2 Corinthians 5:17, If anyone is in Christ, he is a new creature, the**

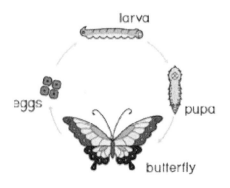

old has gone, the new has come. Becoming a Christian is like waking up from a dream, you blink and the old has disappeared and everything is brand new.

When Jesus Christ comes into our lives, He performs a creative miracle of metamorphosis, an inside out transformation. Our old value systems, relationships and philosophies dissipate and are reconstructed around Christ and His value systems. A perfect example is Saul of Tarsus, who became Paul. His transformation took place on the road to Damascus, when he was blinded by a light, and heard the voice of God say, "Saul, Saul, why are you persecuting me?" **Acts 9:3-18**, recalls the events of Saul's conversion. After being blind for three days, Ananias, a priest, touched him and he recovered his eyesight and became an Apostle of our Lord Jesus Christ. He preached to the Gentiles, bringing salvation to multitudes. That complete transformation in Paul prepared him to become an author of thirteen books in the New Testament.

Change reveals the real true beauty that is hidden inside, marred by an unsightly covering. Our spiritual metamorphosis is the process of upgrading our ability to navigate through life's obstacles while maintaining inner peace, which passes all human understanding. It is one of life's greatest blessings that may creep up on us unawares. The end of the caterpillars' life is what we call a new life, a butterfly. The end of our disasters are viewed as a testimony for others to see and be encouraged by, a mess turned into a message.

His caterpillar lifestyle had expired, he was given angelic wings to fly and expound the Gospel through signs and wonders following. We should not be afraid of change, because in the process we will gain something supernatural.

"The smallest act of kindness is more than the greatest intention."

– *Oscar Wilde*

RETURNING TO THE HEART OF THE MATTER

CHAPTER 3

KINDNESS is the God-magnet which when used will attract the unsavoury, the dregs of society, the pariahs and the lepers. When kind deeds are performed to these people, their lives will be touched positively inspiring a broader group of like-minded people. Touch one and create a ripple effect and change many.

When kindness is given in small doses and at the most unsuspecting time, venue and circumstance, it will infiltrate the hard core of cruelty and melt away all the inhumanity. **The law made nothing perfect, and a better hope was introduced, by which we draw near to God,**

Hebrews 7:19. Unfortunately, the church has shattered the illusions into delusions and driven people away from the house of God, by Bible-thumping those who do not walk the walk and talk the talk. They have not embraced and coached the congregants to turn from the errors of their ways to the perfect ways of God, because of their hypocrisy. That hypocrisy has propelled people into living in limbo, open to the influence of philosophies of the world. Preaching the Word of God may not always return the prodigal children back home, but an extended arm of kindness offering assistance in a time of need will surely bring them back home. The Good Samaritan and the God whom he advocates will effect revolutionary modification. That show of kindness, which is a fruit of the Spirit unearths the beauty that was hidden under layers of hurt and animosity. **God had given us beauty for ashes, Isaiah 61:3.** By sprinkling kindness like confetti, we will impact change from callous to caring, thoughtlessness to thoughtfulness, decadent to moral, hateful to loving and selfish to selfless.

Ephesians 4:22-24 encourages us to put off our former way of life, our old self, which is being corrupted by its deceitful desires; to be renewed in the spirit of our minds; and to put on the new self, created to be like God. Acting spontaneously will gain peoples' confidence and convince them of our humanness and ensure that life has meaning not mere existence. Our spontaneity will win them over to be taught kindness and respect for themselves and others and to influence change. Our display of kindness will initially be sneered at, as a weakness, but later admired as a personal strength and an attribute of God. We get what we give, the Golden Rule in Luke 6:31, states **"that we should do unto others as we would have them do unto us."**

Through KINDNESS we can produce a safe, respectable and productive society. It will be the new beautiful, generating unprecedented modification. We should introduce a culture of KINDNESS, not random acts of kindness.

It will open doors of opportunity for the unloved, rejected and abused to be embraced and accepted. They will be engulfed with unconditional love, (agape love, the God kind of love). **Broken hearts will be healed, Psalm 147:3, hardened hearts softened, Ezekiel 36:26, and the cold-hearted will be warmed.**

The condition of our hearts improves with every act of kindness. Serotonin is released by regulating our mood, by calming us down and making us feel happy. An emotional warmth fills the mind and body. Oxytocin is then produced, making us feel optimistic, confident, empathetic and trustful. Stress, anxiety and depression are reduced. Physically it does the following:

- ♥ It lowers high blood pressure, by releasing nitric oxide into the blood vessels which expands the vessels reducing the pressure.

- ♥ Inflammation which increases the risk for artery plaque to rupture and create blood clots is reduced.

- ♥ Free radicals which affect cholesterol levels, by increasing the risk of heart attacks are limited.

- ♥ Anxiety is reduced. Research showed that those who practised loving kindness felt more connected and less anxious.

- ♥ Mood has improved. After doing something kind, mental health was given a powerful boost. That feeling is called the 'helper's high.'

- ♥ Energy levels are boosted, whenever we give back through volunteering or doing good deeds.

- ♥ Pain is reduced when endorphins are released. It is a natural painkiller. Research has shown that altruistic behaviour can relieve physical pain.

- ♥ It builds lasting relationships and community. When our hearts are kind, we are kind to our neighbours. We build strong bonds in relationships because of our compassion.

Let us lend a helping hand and change the way we feel inside and out, because matters of the heart influence the mind and the body, by changing mindsets and altering our behaviours. Transformation of the nations will begin with one person at a time.

"Life becomes easier and more beautiful when we can see the good in other people."
– Roy T. Bennett

VOICES IN THE WORLD

In the past man looked to the world for answers to their questions, solutions to their problems and ways to achieve wealth, health and positivity. Instead, they have been misled into believing that the broad road with all the merriment, eating, drinking, debauchery and celebrations will lead to happiness. Their eyes had been blinded and brains had been rewired to do despicable things like **"sexual immorality, idolatry, sorcery, orgies, rivalries, divisions, dissensions, fits of anger, enmity, strife, envy, jealousy and drunkenness," Galatians 5:19,20.** Their hearts have repudiated the truth and wisdom of God and accepted the philosophies of man. The man had chosen to believe Charles Darwin, a theologian and naturalist's theory of biological evolution instead of the creation of man by God Himself, **in His image and likeness, Genesis 1:27.**

Friedrich Nietzsche, a German philosopher, essayist, cultural critic and atheist wrote about nihilism, which is the denial of reality or extreme scepticism. His writing on truth, morality, power, consciousness and the meaning of existence has influenced man into believing that God is dead.

The corrective punishment that God teaches, is by the use of a rod. *Proverbs 13: 24,* states that **sparing the rod will spoil the child.** Parents were expected to punish their children when they erred.

 Dr Benjamin McLane Spock believed that spanking with a rod is barbaric, evil, cruel or Neanderthal. *"The Common Sense Book of Baby and Childcare,"* written by Dr Benjamin Spock and published in 1946, advocated that children do not require schedules, discipline and affection. It ushered in a fundamental shift in parenting. He advocated that parents, especially mothers; not to be afraid, but to trust their common sense, and show love and affection to their children instead of constant strict discipline. They were to hug their children and tell them that they were loved, unique and special. Parents had to discipline with words, not corporal punishment. He was considered the corruptor of a generation. The neglect of the wise scriptural universal discipline had presented two generations of haughty, selfish, lazy, rebellious and undisciplined youths and his child committed suicide.

Sigmund Freud, a polymath; a fountain of knowledge, who wore many hats, such as a scholar of religion, a scientist, a physician, a neurologist, psychoanalyst, a teacher and a mentor, stated that "religion is so compelling because it appears to "solve" all the problems of our existence." His theory is that the unconscious mind governs behaviour more than people believe. Psychoanalysis makes the unconscious conscious.

Mohandas Karamchand Gandhi, an Indian religious leader, reformer and lawyer, used his religious power for political and social reform. On his arrival in South Africa, he boarded a first-class train but was thrown out because it was designated for whites only. He began an attack on racial discrimination, by developing the concept of 'Satyagraha (Sanskrit: *Satya:* "truth", *agraha:* "insistence" or 'holding firmly to"). Holding firmly to truth or truth force is a particular form of nonviolent resistance or civil resistance. It is not civil disobedience, but a quiet irresistible pursuit of truth.

Oprah Winfrey, an Afro-American television personality, actress and entrepreneur with a daily talk show called The Oprah Winfrey Show, is one of the richest and most influential women in the USA.

On 17 June 1963, **Madalyn Murray O' Hair** finally convinced the United States Supreme Court to ban public prayer in schools. Teachers were not allowed to lead their classes in prayer, devotional readings from the Bible, or other religious activities. Students, however, were allowed to meet and pray on school grounds privately and not to force others to do the same. For five decades America travelled a road of moral and spiritual decay, resulting in social ills such as bullying, alcoholism, drug addiction, early sexual activity, abortions and school-house shootings. God was removed, and Satan came in to steal, kill and destroy. Ex–President Trump in his office of the president said, "The government must never stand between the people and God." We should surely see a difference. These are some people who have influenced mankind over the years, superseding Biblical values, principles and statutes. Their values and philosophies have dictated our choices, unquestionably. We had followed suit only to later realize, that should not have been the route to follow.

However we have to make our own choices, through our experiences with God; not to be influenced by popular people. Our impact on people through our kind speech and deeds will be far greater than we could ever expect. We have to be a living, walking kindness vessel who does not have to think about it but do it spontaneously. Kindness costs nothing but means everything to everyone who has an encounter with kind people. Being kind does not only have a direct effect on others but also has a positive impact on us as well. Everyone deserves a little bit of kindness, so let us spread it. It is one of the greatest attributes that we have to spread help, charity and beauty. Being kind goes a long way. Remember there is no small act of kindness; however, every act creates a ripple with no logical end. It is a passport that opens doors and fashions friends. It softens hearts and moulds relationships that can last lifetimes. Our unexpected kindness is the most powerful, least costly and most underrated agent of human change, therefore we must go forth and be kind.

We must use our voices for kindness, our ears for compassion, our hands for charity, our minds for truth and our hearts for love.

When we think kind thoughts, it creates profoundness, when we speak kind words it creates confidence and giving kindness creates love. Kindness is the best way to heal oneself. It is the greatest gift that we can bestow upon others. Let us lend a helping hand to the needy, without waiting for a thank you, or an expectation of something in return.

We have to begin by speaking kindly to ourselves, and not being over critical. We have to silence the inner critic who always brings us down. Reverse conversations in our heads that dictate that we are guilty, shameful, worthless, depressed, anxious and have low self-esteem. We must tell ourselves that we have been redeemed from guilt and shame. We are worthy, confident and powerful. When we speak kindly to ourselves consistently, we will experience self-belief, happiness, less stress and confidence. Having a positive mindset, will enhance our positive self-talk and attract positive people and experiences. If we struggle with positive self–talk, we must ask friends and family to write down compliments and reiterate them regularly. Let us hear what others say about us if we can't look beyond our own negative impressions. Be in contact with positive people and avoid negative people; because they will contaminate us.

Love dissolves hate.

Kindness melts cruelty.

Compassion calms passion.

Cooperation evokes love.

– *Brahma Kumaris*

GOD; THE FORGOTTEN NOW REMEMBERED

CHAPTER 5

Let us return to God, our Creator and His users' manual for right living, The Holy Bible. In it, He provides us with Basic Instructions Before Leaving Earth. It is time to evoke godly principles to govern our lives. **We can do all things through Christ, who strengthens us, Philippians 4:13.** We are not controlled by our subconscious, but influenced by what our ears listen to, (Word of God). **Faith comes by hearing the word of God, Romans 10:17.** The Word of God has the power to heal, deliver, redeem, set the captive free, renew our minds and transform our lives. We reiterate what God has been saying to us for nearly two thousand years.

Mankind had become deaf to the godly precepts found in the Bible and had been led astray like lambs to the slaughter. The church has been forgotten, they have accepted intellectual messages and knowledge instead of the revelation of the truth of the Word of God. People question the commission of God, of **going into all the world, healing the sick, preaching the Gospel and casting out devils, Matthew 28:19.**

The Good Shepherd, the Holy Spirit, who lives inside of us is redirecting the spirit of man to follow in the footsteps of God Almighty, by hearing the voice of God. We can affect change through Biblical education because God loves us all the time with an everlasting love, Jeremiah 31:3. His agape love accepts us despite our state of being because His grace and mercy are new every day. He asks us to cast all our cares upon Him, for He cares for us, **1 Peter 5:7.** We will be strengthened and sustained. He promises to unburden and relieve us of our troubles because He is faithful, **2 Thessalonians 3:3.** We are assured that we would be preserved blameless until the second coming of the Lord.

The Z Generation, those born during (1995 - 2014) here is a call for you to seek the face of God and put your trust in Him, instead of technology, who is presently your god. Spend some of the seven and a half hours communing with God instead of only socializing with family and friends. You are multi-taskers, who can work on many different tasks at any given time, especially five screens at the same time. Try using at least one screen for spiritual upliftment. By spending at least fifteen hours on your smartphones, you have been made the first true natives of the digital era.

You are tech-smart, constantly learning and have been endowed with entrepreneurial attributes and are always eager to start new businesses, making it a surety to attend a tertiary institution after high school.

Because of your interactive nature with people, you will readily boost their skills. They will be encouraged to believe that anything is possible. Your cautious nature will be imparted to those you interact with, making them careful with their expenses, saving when they can and being careful of their spending.

Your philanthropist ideologies of wanting to make the world a better place will surely impact society, making it a good place to dwell in. Wait upon God, for a good idea that will be fail-safe, to sustain you and provide opportunities for others too.

A masterpiece is the greatest work of a person, with outstanding creativity, excellence, profundity and workmanship. We are pieces in the hands of a Master Potter, who moulds the clay, to fashion it into a piece of beauty, value and honour. Beauty that is admired and desired to be possessed. Value is sought after with a great price and honour is admired and given.

We are God's Masterpiece, created to perform good actions that God prepared long ago to be our way of life, Ephesians 2:10.

As a Masterpiece, we haven't been created only to be admired, desired and possessed like chattel, but to be a blessing and to impact the lives of those that are fortunate to come into contact with us. We should not only be aesthetically pleasing to the eyes but the heart and mind as well. What the eye perceives, is deposited in the mind as a mental picture and downloaded into the chambers of the heart, which is the seat of emotions. The heart controls our speech, actions, attitudes and character. Let us guard our hearts with much diligence because out of it comes forth the issues of life. As masterpieces, we don't need validation from any medieval guild as evidence of qualification for the rank of master, because God has already validated us. **He has made us vessels of honourable use, set apart as holy, useful to the master's house and ready for every good work, 2 Timothy 2: 21.** We should be ready to take advantage of every opportunity to perform generous and noble deeds, which can transform our personal experiences into universal ones. Who we are may not be acknowledged, but our transformational deeds will receive an acknowledgement, bringing glory and honour to our Creator. Let us shine for the world to see the creative, one-of-a-kind and greatest work of the Master. Our style, technique, balance and harmony will evoke feelings of curiosity and awe, because an encounter with a masterpiece will remain and create an imprint for the rest of one's life.

KINDNESS - THE NEW BEAUTIFUL

Kindness makes you the most beautiful person in the world no matter what you look like.

W e are living in a world that is filled with superficial people, self-centred, entitled and without the milk of human kindness.

Our superficiality forces us to look only at outward appearance such as beauty, poise, the styling of our hair, and adorning ourselves with jewellery and beautiful clothes. The world dictates that our outward appearances are important and that we should do everything to enhance and maintain them. For how long can we maintain that outward beauty, which could fade away and diminish with time. Yes, money and plastic surgery can make us look beautiful on the outside temporarily.

Let us yearn to cultivate the inner beauty, the gentle, gracious kind which is a fundamental necessity for stable emotional health that God delights in. It doesn't matter how pretty or handsome we are on the outside; if we are selfish, greedy, unkind, dishonest and ugly on the inside, it tarnishes us completely, marring the outside beauty. Our inner beauty comes from faith in God because He looks at the heart. No fancy hairdo or make-up can beat a caring heart. Scarred tissue will never be able to hide true inner beauty when they are lending a helping hand to the needy and hurting. Although their outer beauty may have declined, their inner nature is nurtured and renewed daily. Our smile is the best make-up that we can wear, to improve our appearance. We can give it to others, altering the way that they would look. It will cost us nothing but will remind us of what we will get when we give. We will receive a big smile in return, brightening their day and ours. Smiles can heal a thousand. They may hide feelings such as sadness, fear and heartbreak, but it also reveals strength. Share your smile with the world, it will mean a thousand words, and reveal a thousand problems that have been hidden. Let us use our smiles to change the world, don't let the world change our smiles. Phyllis Diller said, "A smile is a curve that sets everything straight." Every day, when we come across people who don't have a smile, please give them one of yours, because it changes their world. Your gentle words, kind look and good-natured smile can work wonders and accomplish miracles.

Sadly, in my interaction with both adults and children, I wonder about their behaviour, common courtesy and kindness. I sometimes ask myself, "Is it so difficult to be kind, good and patient? I inexorably answer my question with, "They are that way, because of who they are, where they come from, and who they interact with daily." People who live unkindly will be unkind. People who are treated with unkindness will treat others with unkindness. Unkind societies will inculcate unkindness in their people, making it their lifestyle. People are what society dictates because they are swayed by social media and examples that are demonstrated at home.

Our display of kindness to them, may initially be regarded as a weakness, and be scorned, but will ultimately become an eye opener of our character, and who we are. My continued kindness has brought about a difference in people's responses. You get what you give.

The 'Golden Rule of Civility' found in **Leviticus 19:18** was quoted by our Lord Jesus in **Matthew 7:12 and Luke 6:31; "Do unto others as you would have them do unto you"**. We can be the primary source of guidance and nurturing of social, emotional and spiritual health. Through kindness, we can produce a safe, respectable and productive society that will not pose a threat, but as a sanctuary. Kindness will become the new beautiful, that will be on exhibition, not only on the playground but in cars, taxis, buses, homes and communities; generating unprecedented modification. **I am convinced and confident of this very thing, that God who has begun a good work in me will continue to perfect and complete it, (Philippians 1:6).**

The Rose Kindness Foundation was created to see God bring about a transformation, where children will not be conformed to the patterns of this world, but be transformed by the renewing of their minds so that they can figure out what God's will for them is, Romans 12:2. Daily, I am confronted with children from different homes, lifestyles, races, creeds and cultures. We congregate to have school, expecting the teacher to adapt to the differences and add her difference, creating what Indians would call, '*breyani*'. Breyani is a mix of a variety of spices, oil, meat, rice, and vegetables cooked together. It is a culinary experience to be savoured, especially at celebrations. Our classrooms have become a cooking pot of emotions and attitudes brought in by every child. The 'troubled', bring in their hurt, rejection, abuse, fear and hate, which meld together as a cacophony but which become music to our ears when they are taught acceptance, tolerance and kindness. These characteristics display their physical, psychological and emotional abuse, wounds and scars through their speech and behaviour. Those who need nursing and nurturing, have to have their wounds bandaged with invisible and physical plasters. Physical ailments are bandaged to bring about healing; while emotional wounds are healed with love and acknowledgement, leaving only scars as a reminder of what had been.

Those who have been chained by strongholds of lies, drugs, alcohol, misconduct and struggles, have created monsters, waiting to emerge. At a mere 'look', a supposed whisper, 'they were talking about me', or not being selected to play; they retaliate with how they know best, they 'BITE', they lash out verbally with the most intense vulgarity, or with outstretched 'claws', to scratch at and be ever ready to kick at. More often than not there's a weapon, a little rock or even stationery which is used to 'defend' themselves and injure others. To them, there is absolutely nothing wrong with their actions. They give as good as they get. That is all that they are familiar with, they receive that torture at home repeatedly and accept it as the norm. Those are the perfect responses perpetrated in their minds at the slightest provocation. Anger is a spiteful attitude of retaliation and revenge.

When that behaviour is on display then we are motivated to respond in anger and extreme rage; but love, respect, patience, kindness and compassion should emerge to eradicate all the hate that is embedded deep inside their soul. Kindness and the other fruit of the spirit, love, joy, peace, patience, gentleness, goodness, and self-control are interrelated; graces of the Spirit which can make a difference. In our demonstration of kindness towards these children, we inevitably extend gentleness, patience and goodness, showing them that this world is not filled with atrocity. The goodness will overlook the bad behaviour, but identify the tiny iota of good that lies hidden beneath the abuse. It is a bountiful inclination to be and do good in the midst of annoyance and is only possible by the grace of God. Gentleness is our disposition of sweetness, tranquillity and affection which stifles the normal human reaction of dismay, and replaces turmoil, revulsion and disapproval. This even temperament leaves us relating to incidents in a pleasant manner, not in a tirade of emotions as most people expect. Injuries are pardoned, faults are rectified and the soul is taught to be ruled by the spirit, not the carnal instinct. In our humanness, we do become annoyed at the repeat offenders, but the benevolence within us will allow us to be well-meaning and assist and serve them in love. The display of the fruit of kindness from us will surely astonish them, causing them to question their behaviour and generate change.

Perseverance will produce not only the fruit from your harvest, but the beauty of blossoms to erase the sorrows in the toiling. Don't give up before you reap the rewards of your labour of love. **Galatians 6:9, Let us not be weary in**

doing well: for in due season we shall reap if we faint not. We have to focus on the treatment of those around us, through the power of God. We should restore the immoral with gentleness and humility. Doing good is not an easy task, especially when people doubt your actions. We should keep on living in a way that is consistent with what we believe, and not be dissuaded by the masses. Our good works will bear fruit, which the next generation will feed off. Our investment in the lives of those around us will yield the best interest in bringing about a new creation.

Change doesn't come easily or from comfort, but from much honing. If it doesn't challenge us it will not change us and others. Relentless practice will reap an abundant harvest. Patience is a key element of success. It teaches that life is a series of natural and spontaneous changes that should not be resisted, because they will bring sor-

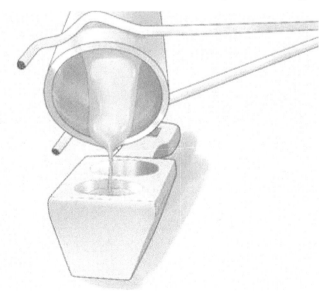

row. If we want to change, we have to be willing to be uncomfortable. We should also be prepared to bear the discomfort in the process. To purify gold, it has to be placed in a furnace for a prolonged period of time. It is only through that refining process that all the impurities are removed and pure gold is produced.

"Kindness changes everything"
– *Tracy Howard*

CHAPTER 7

MY SEARCH AND JOURNEY

I've been searching for that which God had prepared a long time ago within me. In my short-sightedness, I did not perceive that the fullness of the Godhead dwells in me, making me an imitator of Christ, thus making me a model for others to aspire to, and emulate. My life's purpose is to walk, talk and live like the way our Lord did, and to make a difference wherever I go. Lives matter, so we must be challenged to bring about life-altering change, through our speech, actions, attitudes and character.

I've finally come to understand the meaning and purpose of my life. That is to bring out the best in each person whom I interact with, by drawing out their hidden potential that has been concealed, by the prince of the air, through deception and wrong thinking. Embedded deep within the crevices of their hearts and minds are false ideologies that have been spoken repeatedly. "You are good for nothing," "You are useless." "Nothing will come of you." "You will amount to nothing." "You will end up like your useless mum or dad." These are some rhetoric Satan pollutes their mind by making them feel guilty, shameful, unworthy, unloved, unaccepted, unappreciated and uncalled for. The enemy has been successful in deluding people and taking them away from the kingdom, through poverty, lack and procrastination; but he has met his match in me. He has tried to suppress me from my inception, but what God has ordained will supersede all strategies of the enemy. I have a testimony to reveal that God can and will use the base things of this earth to confound the wise, **1Corinthians 1:27.** That He will cause the simple to stand before kings, **Proverbs 22:29.** If God could do that for me, He can do it for anyone.

When I was barely thirteen years old, God had spoken through his servant prophetically, that I would become a teacher. At that time having to attend a tertiary institution was only a pipedream, something only rich people could afford. My future was spoken and declared by God through His servant, Pastor Roderick, and was brought to fruition four years later when I was offered a bursary to study teaching at Springfield College of Education. Kindness was extended to me by my brother-in-law, Bala Kuppusamy, who nurtured and cared for me financially, materially and spiritually when my retired dad could not.

John 10:10, the thief comes to rob, kill and destroy, but God has come to give life and give it in abundance. I am now living that abundant life promised.

This is my biography.

I acquired diplomas in the following:

- Pre -Junior Primary Education: Springfield College of Education
- Higher Education Diploma in Remedial Education: Springfield College of Education
- Educational Management: MANCOSA
- Theology: Teamwork Bible College of South Africa
- Advanced Christian Counselling – with a practice number to Counsel: Faith Bible College Johannesburg

I acquired degrees in the following:

- Bachelor in Christian Counselling UGCSI California, USA
- Masters in Christian Counselling UGCSI California, USA

- Doctorate in Christian Counselling: UGCSI California, USA

- Dissertation Title: "The Ripple effect of Multiple Parenting"

- Doctorate in Searcherdemics – God's Education System: UGCSI California, USA

Appointments

- Principal: New Life Ministries Bible College

- Member of the Academic Council: UGCSI

- Online International Professor: UGCSI

Work Experience

- Foundation Phase Educator

- School Counsellor/Mentor

- Prayer Group Leader

- Head of Department Foundation Phase: Richards Bay Primary School

Clergy Jobs

- Children's Church Teacher & Superintendent

- Women's Group Leader

- Bible Study Teacher
- Intercession Leader
- Preacher
- Biblical Counsellor
- Pioneer & Overseer of Private School: New Life Academy
- Active Member: INKOSI Community Projects
- Annual Youth Day Events: Float processions, fun & games, motivational speakers
- Preparing of banners, feeding schemes, sporting events, sponsorships/fundraising drives
- Founding member of the Rose Kindness Foundation.

The above positions and experiences in my life have birthed the following accolades.

While completing my degree in Theology, I was introduced to Sir Clyde Rivers and Prof. Michal Pitzl, who visited South Africa to bestow an Honorary Doctorate on my pastor Mr Daniel Munsamy. During their interaction with me, I frivolously commented on being the Principal of the UGSCI South Africa.

After a while, nine other members and I were offered a scholarship to study through United Graduate College

and Seminary International. I did become the Principal of UGCSI Richards Bay with twenty-five students completing their studies. After fourteen years of studying, I am now a recipient of a PhD in Biblical Counselling and an online Professor.

On 11 April 2021, I was awarded the African Civility Educator of the Year Award, becoming one of the many icons of change in society.

On 18 May 2021, I was a guest on The Africa Civility Show. It was an awe-inspiring experience that I will never forget. It was an hour of thought-provoking questions and answers.

In my limited experience, I was able to impact the world with nuggets of knowledge to be implemented to bring about change and transformation. If people will put their trust in God and not in man, they will see the benefits of kindness. Kindness is the key to complete transformation

because it is the Golden Rule of Civility. If each of us practices it, we will live in a civil society where we love one another as ourselves. Matthew 7:12, Do unto others as we would have them do unto us.

On 2 April 2022, I was one of three people who was conferred with another doctorate.

It was the first time ever in the history of UGCSI. It was an online graduation.

Doctorate in Searcherdemics-God's Education System.

THE KINDNESS FOUNDATION

It is a Non-Profit-Organisation that has been established to promote kindness in action. It has been established in Richards Bay to take care of the needy, abused and homeless. It will be a place of safety for women and children who are physically, verbally and emotionally abused. They will be accommodated, supported and given therapy before being reintegrated back into society. The premises still have to be purchased. This organisation will rely totally on funding, donations and sponsorship from the public.

Our Mission Statement:

We have Kingdom Integrated Notions for Developing the Nation into Endeavouring Solicitous and Sympathetic citizens.

Our Vision:

We are dedicated to bringing humanity back to God's given purpose of living a fulfilled, accepted, life of civility.

Our Service:

We are not selling any products, but providing a service to the emotionally challenged, ensuring that they overcome their difficulty and are back on their feet as independent individuals. This sets us apart from other industries, because it is humanitarian and altruistic. The dregs of society can be rehabilitated and sent back into society to live normal lives of positive impact. Let us not treat them like lepers, if lepers were touched and healed by our Lord, so can these people too. They can be productive citizens again.

Through the word of my testimony, I was able to draw others to put their trust in a God of the impossible. People who had no hope, studied God's Word, stood upon His promises and declared it over their lives to finally see it manifest itself. They did their best and God did the rest. He opened doors of opportunity that were impossible in the natural realm, but possible in the spiritual realm because they believed and put their trust in God. God had given them the keys to the Kingdom, to unlock doors that were shut to them and to lock doors that the enemy had opened to prevent them from achieving their dreams. The unyielding prayers of mothers was heard and answered. There are students who are now attending universities on full scholarships. Is anything too difficult for God? No, our Lord who is at work in our lives can do the same for you.

Fragile egos have been strengthened to withstand the heat of the furnace and have been proven to be strong pillars for the Lord. As a teacher of the Word of God, I've had to be a sterling example to follow. The Word of God is nourishment to the spirit man, who is growing in leaps and bounds. It is milk to the babies in Christ, and meat to the mature in the church of God. His word is an effective agent to accomplish exactly what He intends. It brings healing, deliverance, provision and promises to fulfilment. We can be confident that what God has spoken will materialize.

The word of God is relational, He spoke to Adam to instruct him in the book of Genesis. He established a covenant with Abraham, He instructed, rebuked and encouraged the prophets who were faithful. The word became flesh and dwelt among men, in our Lord Jesus Christ.

The Bible is God's special revelation to man, to direct us to salvation in Christ, our Messiah. The Bible is our basic instruction for believers to live on earth. It has all the power of God behind it to change our lives.

From childhood, we have known the Holy Scriptures, which has made us wise for salvation through faith. Scripture is profitable for doctrine, for reproof, for correction, for instruction in righteousness and to equip us thoroughly for every good work; because the unfolding of it gives light and understanding to the simple. For the word of God is alive and active and it judges our thoughts and the attitudes of our hearts. It is a lamp for our feet and a light to our paths, shielding all who take refuge in Him. He has promised to keep us from harm, by watching over our lives, both our coming and going. In Corinthians we are told to do everything in love; because love is patient, kind, rejoices with the truth, always protects, trusts, hopes, perseveres and never fails. It is not envious or boastful, is not proud, or self-seeking and does not dishonour others and delights in evil. It is not easily angered and does not keep a record of wrongdoings, but rejoices with the truth. When we let love and faithfulness never leave us, and bind it around our necks and write them on the table of our hearts; we will find favour and a good name in both the sight of God and man. When we live in love, we live in God and He lives in us. We will become completely humble, gentle and patient and bear with one another in love.

SOMETHING TO STRIVE FOR AND LIVE BY DAILY.

"For attractive lips, speak words of kindness.
For lovely eyes, seek out the good in people.
For a slim figure, share your food with the hungry.
For beautiful hair, let a child run his fingers through it once a day.
For poise, walk with the knowledge you'll never walk alone.
We leave you a tradition with a future.
The tender loving care of human beings will never become obsolete.
People even more than things have to be restored, renewed, revived, reclaimed and redeemed and redeemed and redeemed.
Never throw out anybody.

Remember, if you ever need a helping hand, you'll find one at the end of your arm.

As you grow older, you will discover that you have two hands: one for helping yourself, and the other for helping others.

Sam Levenson

IT IS OUR SAFE PLACE TO LEARN AND GROW

WHAT IS THE FRUIT OF KINDNESS?
Galatians 5:23

The fruit of the Holy Spirit is a biblical term that sums up nine attributes of a person living in accordance with the Holy Spirit. The fruit of the Spirit is love, joy, peace, patience, KINDNESS, goodness, faithfulness, gentleness and self-control. The fruit is contrasted with the works of the flesh which immediately precede it in this chapter. The works of the flesh are, sexual immorality, impurity, sensuality, idolatry, sorcery, enmity, strife, jealousy, fits of anger, rivalries, dissensions, divisions, envy, drunkenness and orgies." The works of the flesh and fruit of the Spirit are found in **Galatians 5:19-23.**

- The Greek word *kalosyni* defines kindness as goodness, benevolence, clemency and humanness. It is the grace which pervades the whole nature, mellowing all who would be harsh and austere.

- A tender heart and a nurturing spirit. It could be an impossible goal in our own strength, yet attainable, but not automatic. It is only experienced when we are yielded to the Holy Spirit.

- Kindness is loaning someone our strength instead of reminding them of their weakness.

- Kindness is a matter of putting our own needs aside and simply doing something that we know will be helpful or make someone else feel loved and appreciated.

- Kindness is the quality of being warm-hearted, considerate, humane and sympathetic.

- Kindness is bringing warmth and value to somebody with no expectation in return.

- Kindness is being sympathetic, and helpful and making the world a better place.

- Kindness is the quality of being gentle, caring and helpful.

- Kindness is helpfulness towards someone in need, not for the advantage of the helper, but for that of the person being helped.

- Kindness is stepping out of your world to make someone else better.

- Kindness is the state of being friendly, generous, gentle and considerate.

- Kindness is treating people the way you want to be treated.

- Kindness is having a tender heart with a desire to share generously with others.

- Kindness is recognizing that relationships are core to who we are becoming, and therefore being tender, courteous, helpful, forgiving and compassionate towards others and ourselves.

When we submit ourselves to God and allow Him to take full control of our lives, the flesh is subdued and the nature of God replaces it. The flesh, which includes harsh words, raised voices and intolerance will always try to surface, but the presence of the Holy Spirit in our lives will bring those feelings under control.

I have had several meetings with learners, teachers, parents and managers, where I heard the human souls cry out for help daily in different forms. The naughty ones seek attention in any form, unfortunately, more negative than positive, resulting in fighting, bullying, stealing and dehumanising others. Adults take to backbiting, looking down upon themselves and others, fighting for power, making others' lives miserable and being judgmental. After observing their hunger and thirst for acceptance, compassion and sympathy a fire was kindled inside of my spirit to warm the cockles of those cold hearts, through the healing power of God. He said, **He will heal the broken-hearted, and bind up their wounds Psalm 147:3.**

The fire that can warm those cold hearts is love in action, through kindness. By extending God's grace, mercy and loving-kindness the first step in affecting change occurs. Initially, it will be a kindling, but later becomes a blazing forest fire, that will consume most of the negative attitudes and create an awareness and speculation for the difference that we are making. Enquiries have been made about how a soft approach with the naughty kids, still brings about acceptable behavioural change. The answers given are hate and animosity breeds hate and animosity, but a soft answer turns away wrath, but a harsh word stirs up anger, Proverbs 15:1. Being riled up with disobedient children and screaming and shouting at them will not bring solutions to the problems, but make them even more obstinate. **The tongue of the wise uses knowledge rightly, Proverbs 15:2.** A show of kindness in enquiring about the misdemeanour conducted and not an accusation always provides the different perspectives of the misdemeanour. Getting down to their level of speech and language, to make it comprehensible, crouching in front of them; not being tall, looming and brutish. A gentle smile; immediately invites a state of serenity and security. Answers become forthcoming, lies are eliminated and the truth surfaces.

During discourses with the culprits, their input on the misdemeanour was requested and together we searched for corrective measures to be implemented in the future. That method of investigation brought them to a self-realisation, and a repentant spirit. They were remorseful about their actions and sought forgiveness, with the promise to endeavour to be well-behaved in future. While watching those children from afar during the course of the day, I witnessed the promise for change being implemented. Miracles do not always happen immediately, but continued positive reinforcement will definitely bring about the desired change.

Children who struggle academically and have been labelled by previous teachers as useless, good for nothing will continue to perform at that level. A reminder of their misdemeanours will only corroborate their unacceptable behaviour as normal.

When children are given a little extra attention, complimented for their good performances; and encouraged to try a little harder, they will put in a little more effort, to make a change, even a miniscule bit. My motto of, **"We can do ALL things through God, who gives us the abil-**

ity," **Philippians 4:13,** can become theirs as well. The daily declarations of our belief will become evident in the extra effort put in, the radiance on their countenance when they receive their results after an assessment, with passing grades. A new sense of confidence will originate within, causing them to step out of their shell of fear and rejection and rise up with pride as eagles. They will be able to hold their heads up high with self-assurance and poise. They will find their place in the classroom, on the playground and finally in society. They will not be left in the shadows as unseen, and unknown individuals, but as children with a purpose. That self-confidence will give them a voice, not making them social outcasts, but parts of groups that are accepted and included in activities.

Children with low self-esteem about their appearance can be made to realise that they have been created in the image of God, **Genesis 1:26.** If they have been created in God's image, then they are not 'ugly', they are beautiful, yet different. They are beautiful in their uniqueness. Those who wear spectacles and suffer with an inferiority complex, are repeatedly teased, "four eyes' feel unattractive, but with constant reminders of how pretty or handsome they are, they will accept their inner and outward beauty. They will come to realise that some of us have shortfalls or lack in certain areas of our lives and that can be rectified by wearing spectacles, hearing aids, walking with a crutch, being pushed in a wheelchair or using an inhaler to help them breathe properly. They are dissimilar, but special in their own uniqueness. We will no longer see hangdog looks of disappointment and rejection, but smiles of self-assurance. Their beauty that was distorted and hidden from their view under all the ash has now been revealed, **Isaiah 61:3**. Their eyes will open to admire the innate beauty that God placed within them. Continued positive reinforcements and re-affirmations will completely eradicate their low self-esteem. These children when given opportunities to do different activities such as being the class captain, chalkboard cleaner and runner will bolster their skills. Create opportunities for them to succeed, thereby boosting their confidence. When called cool names, they would live up to the image. Names such as Smarties, Super Sleuths, Clever Cats and My Brain Boxes. Compliments enhance their self-esteem and boost their morale. A positive sense of self makes them competent and develops them into happy productive beings. Public praise and private constructive criticism will cause them to be prepared to rectify the wrong and seek after that which is right. Be available for them when they require assistance, show them that they are not alone, that we are there walking alongside them.

We have to mentor, without walking ahead to show the way and how things were done, but walk alongside and show what can be done. A truly great mentor is hard to find, difficult to part with and impossible to forget. Take a hold of those little hands, lead, guide, direct and encourage their minds to think, hands to create and hearts to love. The influence of a kind individual cannot be erased; it will remain for a lifetime. Our kindness affects eternity, and we can never tell where our influence stops.

When seeds of kindness are sown, they will grow forever, from one generation to the next; pushing roots deeper and deeper into the ground for stability and producing beautiful blossoms and bearing delicious fruit. Let us become kind teachers, who are compasses that navigate the magnets of curiosity, knowledge and wisdom in the children we teach, by magically transforming facts and figures into inspiration and wisdom. Let us become the teachers, who are inspirational individuals who create future game changers. To the world, you may be a teacher, a parent, a sibling, or a relative, but to individuals, you are a mentor, a friend, a listening ear, a kind heart, a shoulder to cry on and a hero. Heroes who don't wear capes and masks, but a beautiful smile, extending a hand of generosity, and a warm embrace. Our merciful, gracious, tender and kind temperament will be an open door of acceptance when the world closes around them. Let us be the safe haven for those lost in the storms of life, with their myriad challenges. Through our kindness, we can make people feel most beautiful in this ugly world despite what they look like.

Let us do the following:

- Speak without accusing.
- Listen without interrupting.
- Give without sparing.
- Promise without reneging.
- Answer without arguing.
- Share without being selective.
- Enjoy without complaining.
- Forgive without punishing.
- Trust without wavering.
- Help without a reward.
- Volunteer without any expectations.
- Send get well cards.
- Donate to charity.
- Provide meals to the hungry.
- Clothe the naked.
- Protect the weak.
- Reduce risk.
- Eradicate bullying.
- Be a safe haven.
- Love without judging.
- Pray for them without ceasing.

BREAKING THE BARS THAT HOLD US BOUND

W e were created with innate goodness, which stems from the virtues of God, our Creator. These virtues include a proper mind, a healthy emotion, and a strong will which manifests itself in love, light, holiness and righteousness. When we are overly exposed to our free will and not the mind of Christ, our minds and hearts become the battleground between good and evil. We experience battles in our thoughts, which we have to diffuse and defeat. If not defeated, they become mental strongholds, which keep us shackled. Strongholds of the mind are lies that have been established in our thoughts, which we believe as truth because we are familiar with them as part of our cultural beliefs. Those lies affect our attitudes, emotions and behaviour. When we are given choices, we are empowered, and develop problem-solving skills, which can be utilized when the need arises. When the potential inside each one is realised, then we are able to drive it out by breaking the moulds that held us captive in our minds.

God wants us to walk in victory and freedom in our thought-life because the truth will set us free. When we partner with our Lord, enter into worship and embrace our kingdom identity as children of God, we will be victorious. The word of God will help us identify thought patterns that can become strongholds and teach us how to break them. We can demolish strongholds by replacing them with freedom from the word of God. It is an active and intentional lifestyle whereby we fill up on truth in our minds, and hearts and live it out in our decisions and actions. We break the power by becoming open books for the world to read, exposing the lies of the enemy. The enemy will return to tempt us away time and again, but when we are filled with the fullness of God, the Holy Spirit will alert our conscience to prevent us from reverting to our old thought patterns and from being rebuilt as strongholds of the mind. We will be able to take every thought captive so that selfish emotions will not rule.

Mental strongholds have been broken, releasing us from generational curses that held us bound mentally, spiritually, physically and materially. We were redeemed from the curse of the law when our Lord hung on the cross,

Galatians 3:13.

Mental strongholds are thoughts and ideas that were downloaded from generation to generation as belief systems through superstitions, old wives' tales and generational practices. We are captivated and governed by those belief systems, and build our values around them, inadvertently training the next generation. Superstitions and myths become a lifestyle, with the misconception that something evil would occur if transgressed. Old wives' tales, feng shui, mythology, traditions, legends and folklore is passed down as truth. Embedded in these belief systems are cults, demonic powers, rituals, mantras and lies which hold us behind bars in mental captivity. Whatever has had a stranglehold of us in our minds, is destroyed through new godly thought processes. When we think and meditate on things that are true, noble, just, pure, lovely, of good report, virtuous and praiseworthy, Philippians 4:8, there will definitely be a breaking of strongholds, because we are replacing them with the truth. Our minds will be bound to the mind of Christ, and whatsoever we bind on earth will be bound in heaven, and whatsoever we loose on earth, will be loosed in heaven, because we possess the keys to the kingdom, Matthew 16:19. Doors that are shut from the enemy will always remain locked, not allowing them entry into the mind and heart of God's people. Those thoughts and idealism that kept us under the yoke of bondage will break under the power of the Holy Spirit.

We are now **refugees of the LORD, Psalm 9:9**; who builds a new defensive structure around us, protecting us in times of trouble and from being oppressed. God becomes our refuge, high tower and fortified place to run to. He will surround us like the mountains surrounding Jerusalem. This is manifested daily in our lives by being educated and disciplined by the Word of God. We can break through every thought that holds us captive in our mind, which is the battlefield. The truth can expose and destroy the errors and sins that exist in our lives, by looking to Jesus, who is the Way, Truth and the Life. He will reveal who we are through His word. We are set free; we are no longer slaves to sin; but children of God. That knowledge will enable us to cast down arguments and every high thing that exalts itself against the knowledge of God and to bring every thought into captivity to the obedience of Christ. **The weapons of our warfare are not carnal but mighty in God for pulling down strongholds, 2 Corinthians 10:5,4.**

We are in total control of our minds, we can defeat evil thoughts by meditating on the Word of God, thinking on thoughts that are honest, just, pure, lovely and of good report.

We have the ability to switch thoughts that are depressive to thoughts of encouragement and edification like we switch channels on remote control. We have to grab every thought and subject it to God through His Word. We are commanded to take every thought captive, not to let our thoughts captivate us.

During the battle, soldiers wore a helmet to protect them from damaging and deadly blows to the head. Spiritually we are instructed to wear the helmet of salvation in **Ephesians 6:17.**

It is a protective armour that we have to wear to ward off deceptive, debilitating and destructive thoughts as mental attacks of the enemy disorient, discourage and destroy us. The helmet of salvation gives us hope, which is an anchor for the soul which is sure and steadfast; giving us stability and the ability to weather the worst storms. This hope motivates and sustains us throughout our lives. It gives us hope in the worst circumstances, enabling us to fight against despair and discouragement.

We get to take captive every thought to make it obedient to Christ, **2 Corinthians 10:5**.

We are at war with false teachings, which invade our minds and hearts daily. We do not fight with physical weapons, but with spiritual ones, constantly doubting our knowledge. The tools that we use are prayer and scripture which are powered by God.

They are potent to destroy strongholds of resistance and help us fix our minds on things that are pure, holy and on Christ. We must be able to destroy arguments, philosophies, opinions, perceptions, pretension and self-talk which are against the knowledge of God. Wrong teaching leads to incorrect thinking, which eventually leads to disobedience and walking away from God. Understanding the knowledge of God, will bring our hearts and thoughts to be aligned with Christ's, leading us to right thinking, and finally to obedience and back to God. Every thought conceived and every imagination that invades our minds must be taken captive and then put under the authority of God. Thoughts of God and His word will eradicate the influence of the world view. The more we dwell on the Lord Jesus the less we think of ourselves.

"Your mind is a garden.
Your thoughts are the seeds.
You can grow flowers, or you can grow weeds."

– Tamara Kulish

DISCIPLED BY THE WORD OF TRUTH

What is discipline? Discipline really means to instruct, educate, prepare, regulate, teach and train oneself to develop self-control. Self-control is the ability to think about one's words and actions and how they would affect others. It is the magic power that makes one unstoppable. It is knowing the rules and applying them to avoid facing the consequences.

When we know the rules and refuse to follow them, then we become inconsiderate of others around us; leading to negative connotations of correction, punishment and chastisement. When disobedience is displayed and not rectified it will bring pain, embarrassment and humiliation. Discipline is not mean, embarrassing, or punitive and does not destroy one's sense of worth. It will develop one's internal ability to guide one's behaviour and actions in proper ways in every situation. This should begin in childhood. **Train up your child in the way he should go; and when he is old, he will not depart from it, Proverbs 22:6.** We have to train our children today; because tomorrow may be too late. We should not waste a single day, because we do not have forever. They will quickly grow beyond our training and influence. Yes, our efforts to train and chasten them will surely provoke them, but if not done, it will lead them astray.

Children are given to us helpless and open to instruction, during a window of time to be trained. It has to be done then, before that window of opportunity is closed. Child training and chastening have to be done early in their lives and firm enough to cause proper pain, without compromise for foolish parental pity or tearful appeals by the child. Child training is not an option, but a commandment. Ephesians 6:4, Fathers, do not provoke your children to anger but bring them up in the discipline and instruction of the Lord.

Hannah delivered Samuel to Eli right after his weaning. He was prepared to live away from home, follow instructions and worship God from a very early age. When we begin at an early age, then later we will only have to remind them. Self-discipline is a key virtue that can be effectively taught. True parental love will always find creative ways to accomplish much early enough. Every year left untrained makes it difficult to change habits and attitudes.

Chastening is God's method for training our children for godly and successful lives, which has to be done early. When we wait too long children become hardened in rebellion, establish their own thoughts, form their own habits, resent correction and leave home and live on their own.

Training our children is not an option but a commandment. **Proverbs 23:13**, do not withhold discipline from a child; if you punish them with the rod, they will not die. Chastening is the use of punishment to produce pain for the enforcement and reinforcement of training. It is corrective punishment for them; to visit with an affliction for moral improvement.

Discipline changes with the age of children; the younger they are the more guidance is required. It is a way to protect them from hurting themselves. We have to discipline and guide our children's behaviour respectfully, firmly and matter-of-factly even when we feel anxious or angry. **We have to remain in control, be angry but sin not, Ephesians 4:26.** Discipline has to be consistent with boundaries set and consequences followed.

With older children, discipline is a way to nurture safe and acceptable behaviours and moral principles. Different approaches to discipline have to be used for different children. Teenagers are disciplined with guidance when they make mistakes or unwise decisions. While disciplining, we have to always let them know that we still love them. Children who are disciplined with love will demonstrate kindness wherever they go. They will do unto others as it was done to them.

Biblical discipline clearly indicates that God disciplines those He loves and chastens every child of His, Hebrews 12:6. Children are chastened for their profit so that they can become holy. Children are disciplined to do that which is pleasing and acceptable without harming others. **Hebrews 12:11, states that no discipline seems pleasant at the time, but painful. Later on, however, it produces a harvest of righteousness and peace for those who have been trained by it.** It is short-term pain, but long term gain.

To discipline a child is to produce wisdom, but a mother is disgraced by an undisciplined child, Proverbs 29:15. If we shrink back from our discipline we will be destroyed, but if we persevere we will receive all that God promises. Disciplined lives reap rewards. It is an expression of love because we seek the child's best interest. When disciplined children remark that they don't love us, remind them that now they don't love us, but will be grateful later on. We have to give warnings before acting. Children need to understand that there are consequences to their actions. We have to be consistent in our discipline, and not want to be our children's friends. The goal of discipline is to teach obedience, which will eventually become self-discipline.

The interruption of domestic tranquility for a few minutes now is much less than the calamity that will come with it later. We should not let anything distract us or stop us from this sober equation.

They may kick and scream and throw a tantrum to avoid discipline. If we ignore that now we will save a lot of tears later. **True love is not just hugs and kisses, but correction; withholding correction is hatred, Proverbs 13:24**. If we truly love our children, we will want their very best in a functional and prosperous life. That will only come with discipline.

Eli compromised his sons and brought infinite pain to his entire family. He ignored his sons' infractions and character flaws to have peace. It was an ungodly pity that hindered him from doing his duty for their happiness and good. His poor parenting and lack of discipline resulted in trouble at home and country. He tried to live vicariously through his sons and enjoyed their ill-gotten gains from them. His unrestrained behaviour did not teach wisdom but allowed for growth in foolishness and no fear for God. Eli allowed his sons to self-destruct and be condemned by God. He also allowed untold hurt to be visited upon an entire community, where 30000 men died. **1 Samuel 2**.

Undisciplined children become like Jacob, a cheat and a liar; who end up running for the better part of their lives. They may not be fortunate to have an encounter with our Lord, who changes their names and character. Discipline today and they will become disciples.

DISCIPLINE is doing what you know needs to be **DONE,** even when you don't want to do it.

www.barbelsandbeans.com

"Be mindful. Be grateful. Be positive.
Be true. Be kind."
– Roy T. Bennett

WHAT IS EDUCATION?

"Education is the wise, hopeful and respectful cultivation of learning, whereby everyone has a chance to share in life,"

– Mark K. Smith.

It is an investment in the lives of children, which goes beyond skills, knowledge and understanding of content and curricula. It is opening the mind's eyes to see; the ears of the heart to listen and granting confidence to the mouth to speak.

"Education is the process of facilitating learning, or the acquisition of knowledge, skills, values, morals, beliefs and habits," *Wikipedia.* Children do not only learn what they hear, but what they see on display daily. They will emulate teachers because teachers are supposed to know it all.

Children are stimulated mentally and physically, they are taught to read, write and do mathematics. They receive systematic instruction that would later make them independent. Later they are invited into truth and possibility by making deposits of knowledge into their banks of cognition. Those deposits encourage them to discover the process of living, developing and bringing out their potential. It is the most critical investment made. Nelson Mandela, our late President said, "Education is the most powerful weapon which you can use to change the world." It is the key to eliminating gender inequality, reducing poverty, creating a sustainable planet, preventing needless deaths and illnesses and fostering peace. It is understanding, leading, guiding and directing children developmentally, intellectually, emotionally and spiritually.

It is teaching children how to think and preparing them to be successful in a challenging and competitive world.

"In our knowledge economy, education is the new currency by which nations maintain economic competitiveness and global prosperity. It is feeding our minds with information, making us academic geniuses, who do not influence the person, human being," F. A. Von Hayek. We exist, we do not live. We are not being. We have to be real people, who are governed by our hearts and emotions, not robots; who are uploaded with data to perform certain actions without thought. Education is not only teaching us to read, write and count, it is instilling life skills to lead a fulfilled life of worth.

We are expected to be equipped to live life with all the challenges thrown at us. That equipment comes from the Word of God, which is the users' manual for an accomplished life.

The Basic Instructions for life Before Leaving Earth is enclosed within these pages. (BIBLE)

The mysteries of God were hidden in the Old Testament times and only revealed through the prophets sent by

Him. The entire Bible is the revelation of God's mystery in Christ. **All things were made by Him for Him, Hebrew 13:8.** "The Bible is the only completely trustworthy source of knowledge about God." We can't learn everything about God from human reasoning, philosophy or experiences.

He alone is the source of the knowledge about Himself; through His word, The Bible. By reading the Bible, knowledge replaces ignorance.

It takes the night to express the glory of day. The vessel of dishonour reveals the love and care for the vessel of honour. The evil, immoral women sell their morals to express the virtue of a decent genuine lady. The thief conveys the genuineness of a real Christian and a hypocrite to show up a believer.

We should make our identification with Him because He has identified Himself with us, not only through confession, but by living like Him. When God left, He did not leave us destitute, but left Holy, unique and His perfect design. Psalm 139:14 bears testimony to this, "We are fearfully and wonderfully made." God is not an author of confusion, but order and perfection. He created each of us to be deserving of an education that would enhance us and how we learn. Each of us has our different levels of thought processes because we are provided with opportunities to use creative thinking, higher order thinking, critical thinking, problem-solving and basic knowledge.

We should be confident and look at the bigger picture and lean not on our own knowledge and understanding, but place our dependence on God Almighty; then only will education become relevant and satisfying.

Education is changing to become more deliberate and hopeful where we are taught to be and do more. It is grounded in the desire that all will flourish and share in life. It has to be a cooperative and inclusive activity to help us live as best as we can. Here hopeful environments and relationships for learning are cultivated. Education is deliberate with a purpose to develop and understand, judgment and enabling action. That is called self-education. It is not curriculum based but provides life skills. Hope is provided, because it is akin to energy, curiosity, to the belief that things are worth doing.

Hope, emotions, intellectual activity, choices and intentions allow us to make wise decisions. Emotions are outgoing and trusting our mood towards the environment. As a choice hope is a theological virtue which accompanies faith and love in 1 Corinthians 13:13. And now these three remain: faith, hope and love. But the greatest of these is love.

Education as an intellectual activity which promotes affirmative courses of actions. As an intention it involves engagements with others and the world, making us more informed, wise and respectful. It is helping us make good judgment about situations. The key word is empirical learning, where we draw insight from our experiences.

We acquire wisdom by developing the capacity to reflect, become knowledgeable and discerning.

Education is a continued capacity for growth, where there is change for the better and sensitivity to improve our lives. It is concerned with who we are, what we value, and our capacity to live life to our fullest; by impacting others positively. Education instils kindness in us. It becomes a natural part of our day, not something extra that we have to fit in. Our greatness is measured by our kindness, our education and intellect by our modesty. A good education can change anyone. It is painful, continual and difficult. It is work done in kindness, by watching, by warning, by praising, but above all by example. So let us lead by example

"Educating the mind without educating the heart, is no education at all."
– Aristotle

Knowledge

Introduces

Notions and

Designs

Necessary for

Essential

Successful

Stewardship

DISCOVERING HIDDEN POTENTIALS

"Having the capacity to develop into something in the future."

After much introspection after dealing with children with defiance and conduct disorders, it impressed upon my heart to create something that will change our perspectives of these children. The change in perspective has to influence our speech, actions, demeanour and eventually our lifestyle. My passion is to see change, reformation and

transformation through the Spirit of God. The world system is advocating an eye for an eye, a tooth for a tooth, but God is using me to bring change by architecting the future. The driving force that catapulted me into developing this programme was, Philippians 1:6, "Be confident that He who began a good work in you will bring it to completion." God will not start something that He cannot complete. It may not be according to our calendar or expectations, but He will work with us and on us to bring the assignment to completion. It is like salvation from sin, which occurs immediately, but the change is a process. It cannot happen overnight unless it is a miracle. When God puts His finishing touch on our lives, we would become a vision to behold.

There is also a promise that "God is working in us, giving us the desire and the power to do what pleases Him," Philippians 2:13. This desire cannot be achieved overnight, there will be many levels of change before a complete turnaround. There is no instant gratification; excellence comes from sheer hard work, patience, endurance and relentlessness. It involves an extensive dedication of time, energy and passion. Numerous methods of change had already been implemented, but with disastrous consequences. Change does not always come easily, but with our repertoire of godly methods, there will be a gradual progression before we will finally experience success. Relapses are part of the transformation process, but with unyielding faith, we can pursue without ceasing to achieve success and significance. Failure is a lesson learned. It is part of life. If you don't fail, you don't learn. if you don't learn you will never change. Henry Ford said," Failure is simply the opportunity to begin again, this time more intelligently."We have to remember that every failure is a step to success. Morihei Ueshiba says that "Failure is the key to success: each mistake teaches us something."

Myles Munroe said that "Failure is not the absence of success. Failure is the neglect of trying." We are human and will err, only God is divine and without sin. So when we do fail, we need to pick ourselves up, dust off and move on. We should not let failure define us, because it is not the end of the journey, only part of it.

Let us not look at failure as the opposite of success but as part of the process. God breathed His breath into man, giving him all of His attributes, so if we as mankind take the time to look deep within ourselves, we will find the genius who is hidden under the clutter of hopelessness, rejection and constant suppression.

Although we may have to wait a while, we need not despair, but always ensure that during our communication our voices and faces agree with our words; because that speaks volumes. "Don't become weary in doing well, because in due season we will reap the benefit," Galatians 6:9. We must never give up on ourselves because the end is always near. Patience and persistence will cause it to materialize. When we powerfully push to reach our full potential our life's purpose will eventually manifest itself to the world. We have to believe in our infinite potential, and not set limitations on ourselves.

We have to unleash our potential, by seeking every opportunity to make a difference.

Potential is a priceless treasure like gold. We all have gold hidden within, but we have to dig to get it out. It is endless, therefore we have to do whatever it takes to unearth it. Confucius said, "We have to inculcate these keys to reach our full potential: the will to win, the desire to succeed and the urge to reach our full potential." We can do that by surrounding ourselves with people who dream, do, believe, think and see the greatness within us, even when we cannot see it ourselves. Let us envision our future and our potential, not our past and mishaps. Eradicate fear and self-doubt because it is the greatest enemy of achievement. Meditating and verbalising that we have more potential than we think will fulfil itself before we know it because what we speak and hear will become a reality.

Jean Van't Hul, echoed that, "Children are naturally creative. It is our job to give them the freedom, materials and space to let their creativity bloom to its fullest potential." Let us not be instruments of suppression, oppression and repression, but become the harvesters of the fruit of our positive influence. When children are told that they are braver than they believe, stronger than they seem and smarter than they think, they will live by those words defying their surrounding expectations. Every child is endowed with unknown power which can surprise us and guide us to a radiant future. It is our influence and task to promote it and make success of it. We should aim to be better than we were yesterday.

"Free the child's potential,
and you will transform him into the world."
– Maria Montessori

THE EFFECTS OF KINDNESS IN MY COUNTRY

CHAPTER 13

"Unity in diversity," is our miraculous motto. People who are looked at and treated as equals immediately react with a positive attitude. We are no longer looked at as the dark continent. We are redeemed of ignorance, inexperience and illiteracy. We have the light of our Lord Jesus Christ shining in and through us. All the darkness around us has been dispelled. **"We are the light of the world," Matthew**

5:14. A city on a hill cannot be hidden. Every tiny light of love and acceptance has created a floodlight of liberation. That which was held back from the have-nots is now easily accessible to all. There is an equal opportunity, allowing everyone to partake of what the Lord of all creation has available. The light of the Lord has illuminated our minds and removed the stronghold of darkness.

We are no longer shackled by the chains of discord, hatred, inhibition and apartheid.

Acknowledging that we have been created in the image of God and are equal; with the same abilities and capabilities, not only puts a smile on our lips but a beam on our faces and joy in our hearts. That radiance of light shines through in our actions, speech and lifestyle of acceptance and camaraderie. Our God-given potentials are being realised and effectively engaged to influence transformation in others with similar circumstances.

People who were oppressed exhibit negativism, anger, hatred, threats and violence. Those pathologically, inherited behaviour had created barricades separating people into cultural, language and racial groups. In real-time those barricades have been crumbling down like the walls of Jericho. All children and adults are treated with the same dignity and respect, despite their creed, colour or culture.

There is no longer a wall of segregation; equality is the principal ingredient in unifying everyone.

Children who display offensive behaviours because of baggage carried from the past are identified and rectified immediately. Nobody is allowed to belittle anyone because of their past experiences. Cultural differences are not sneered at but learned and understood. Inappropriate behaviour is suspended positively in a matter-of-fact manner and corrective measures are implemented. No embarrassment, victimisation, guilt and defensiveness are induced, but life's lessons are attained.

Positive and non-judgmental tones are used when speaking to people from different backgrounds. No one is slighted or talked down to. Education is rectifying defensive behaviours and empowering us. Misinformed and uninformed attitudes are realigned with the attitude of Christ. We are taught to train and redirect our defeating thoughts to positive and triumphant ones. An attitude of gratitude, not vengefulness, is raising our altitude. We do not let anyone's ignorance, hate, drama or negativity stop us from being the person we were created to be. A tiny jot of greatness in our attitude creates a great moment, which becomes a great day, a great week, a great month, a great year and finally a great life.

We are taught miscellaneous strategies to reduce defensiveness; privately after establishing a good rapport with them. We have to be attentive and listen to their reasoning, before invading their belief system with Godly principles. Many South African children have absent fathers and are raised single-handedly by the females and matriarchs of the family. Therefore, they have to experience the father-child relationship through us before they can have an encounter and build trust with an unseen Heavenly Father.

These open lines of communication provide opportunities for dialogue, understanding and perception. Lessons taught include making mistakes because mistakes reveal that learning is occurring, and they are not being judged. We learn more from our failure than from others' success; because failure is not the opposite of success, but part and parcel of success. It doesn't stop us but encourages us to start over repeatedly, building character. The legendary Albert Einstein is quoted as saying, "A person who never made a mistake never tried anything new. We are on this journey of self-discovery, climbing out of pitfalls and up mountainous terrain only to reach our destination a better, learned human being touching lives as we explore through uncharted waters. Obstacles and hurdles challenge us to forge ahead undefeated, touching lives unintentionally." The homeless are taken care of, by having shelters provided. The church provides meals and groceries to sustain them.

Orphans are nurtured at orphanages; foster care facilities provide a safe haven for children of abuse and a stipend is paid to mothers without financial support for their children.

A list of charitable organisations that lend a helping hand in South Africa:

- The Gift of the Givers-Serving Humanity
- Human Rights Institute of South Africa
- The Viva Foundation of South Africa
- MIET Africa-The Adolescent Girls and Young Women Programme
- Save the Children South Africa
- Read Educational Trust
- The South Africa Red Cross Society
- World Vision South Africa- Helps vulnerable children overcome poverty.
- CHOSA- Gives hope to the children of South Africa
- Aids Foundation South Africa

EFFECTS OF KINDNESS, IN OUR EVERYDAY LIFE

People in every walk of life are hungry for acceptance, affection, compassion, sympathy and consideration. Everyone has a story to tell, a life to live; which may not be according to our norms and standards. However, we are expected to live according to God's norms and standards, which demonstrates His unconditional (agape) love. The love with which He gave His only begotten Son, to lay down His life for us, **John 3:16.** Our examples are making the world a better place; one person, one day at a time. Kindness is being sprinkled around wherever we go as confetti, beautifying our surroundings. **Ephesians 4:32,** says, "be kind to one another, tender-hearted, forgiving one another as God in Christ forgave us." Heeding that call of God makes us affectionate, kind and forgiving, and in so doing making a positive change. Eyes are opened to the continuous acts of kindness being performed hourly, daily, weekly, monthly, and annually. Random acts of kindness, have now changed to continual acts of kindness. People are now bringing light to the darkness around us and calming the storms with peace and tranquillity. We are peacemakers after our Heavenly Father's attribute, **Matthew 5:9, blessed are the peacemakers.** With kindness as the leading attribute we are able to solve conflict through negotiations and mediations instead of agitating and confusing people into greater turmoil and strife.

We find that children are kinder to each other, bullying is being reduced, and more love is being spread abroad. Tolerance and acceptance are the mainstay of classrooms, playgrounds, sports fields and communities. What we are sowing is what we are reaping, **Galatians 6:7.** Just as quickly as evil is identified, pleasant, gentle and benevolent mannerisms are displayed when rectifying unacceptable behaviour. The response to this new attitude is an eye-opener to the brazen and callous, who are belligerent after reprimands instead of remorseful.

Acts of kindness are modelled by both adults and children alike. Embracing our diversities with the all-encompassing love of God is making the difference. Simple acts performed daily are transforming our Bethlehem, Judea, Samaria and finally the outer parts of the world will experience it. Love is a verb; we have to DO love. Kind was always regarded as a noun, but we are changing it into a verb as well. Just as we do love, we are doing acts of kindness. We are touching the leper, accepting the hypocrite, being merciful to the ostracised, extending grace to the outcasts and embracing the pariah. **Matthew 11:28, come unto me all who are burdened and heavy laden, I will give you rest,** is becoming our motto. We can and will do greater things than what our Lord did, **John 14:12.** We will unburden them of the heavy yokes that they are carrying, through the mighty word of God. Teaching them to cast their cares to the Lord, who is their burden bearer, will cause them to walk with their heads held high in godly pride and not shame. Taking time to provide for needs, listening to them and not judging them will create relationships of trust and security. They will be rescued, restored and redeemed from themselves and the challenges that overcome them.

When these hierarchies of needs are met, then self-actualisation can take place. "Self-actualization," according to Maslow's hierarchy of needs, is the highest level of psychological development, where the personal potential is fully realized after the basic bodily needs have been fulfilled." Wikipedia. People develop their talents and potentialities which drive them to find meaning and purpose in their lives. They can learn to develop compassion, live authentically and spontaneously, practice acceptance and appreciate the small things in life and finally say, "We have lived."

After taking care of their basic physiological and safety needs, friendship, love, belonging, respect and self-esteem will develop. When people belong they acquire self-esteem, give and receive respect and recognition, creating an earnest desire to become the best that they can be, to fulfil their God-given potential. They become kind human beings.

People who are treated kindly, go out to treat others likewise. Kindness begets kindness. Acts of kindness and generosity makes people feel good, releasing oxytocin, which is a feel good chemical. It is related to the warm feelings and connectedness we have with each other, friendship, love and relationship. It binds human beings together, like the bonding agents between mothers giving birth. It feels good when we do something nice for someone. It also feels good when someone does something good for us. It is Mother Nature's way of getting us to look after each other, through the eyes of loving kindness and mercy. Genuine kindness does not expect anything in return.

The Richards Bay Primary School Kindness Tree is a constant reminder that acknowledges kind acts performed by teachers and learners daily. Names of people who perform acts of kindness are emblazoned on this life-size tree displayed on the wall of a building at the entrance to our school. The leaves and insects that beautify the tree have names written on after the kind acts are brought to my attention. Each learner is rewarded with a lollipop to thank them for remembering to be kind.

"Attitude is a choice.
Happiness is a choice.
Optimism is a choice.
Kindness is a choice.
Giving is a choice.
Respect is a choice.
Whatever choice you
make makes you.
Choose wisely."

– Roy T. Bennet

KINDNESS AND THE FUTURE FROM A BIBLICAL PERSPECTIVE

The Searcher Philosophy, which I have adopted through my studies at United Graduate College and Seminary International has empowered me to contribute to society; beginning at my workplace, Richards Bay Primary School with the children whom I teach and oversee.

1.   I aim to return men and women back to the user's manual; the Holy Bible. That will create God-fearing people who will not be ashamed of the Gospel. When the world fails to provide solutions to challenges, they will come to us who are Number One; with Godly solutions. Unanswered questions will be answered by us the Search-

ers, who are dependent and led by the Holy Spirit. People who are held captive in their minds will have those invisible bars bent and broken by the words and actions of the Most – High God, through us. Man will return to his Maker, who pieced together every cell, every drop of blood and every bone to make them complete and beautiful; a Masterpiece.

What God deposits to us, as Searchers, will be weapons in the hands of future generations defeating the schemes of the enemy and architecting their future with new untouched trends that would be sought after by all. Those who thought that they had reached their demise, with no hope or optimism, have new paradigm shifts, the transformation from the inside out, a true metamorphosis will emerge, transforming 'human caterpillars' into beautiful 'human butterflies' into flights of human kindness. Hope, which is an anchor to the soul, Hebrews 6:19, will be their security, holding them fastened to the seabed, not left to float around in the wind, storms and doctrines of this world. When they are buffeted by the challenges that life throws at them they will have an assurance that their souls are attached to Jesus, who will never leave nor forsake them. They will be guided to safety, security and salvation by anchoring their faith in our Lord Jesus Christ.

A new generation of people will emerge with a positive mind-set of confidence, hope and assurance, because God is in control of their lives, going before us to prepare the way. The veil has been rent, the scales have been removed, opening the eyes of our hearts to see what God has in store for us. **We are no longer conformed to the patterns of this world but are transformed by the renewing of our minds, Romans 12:2**. Our former conduct has changed from corruption and orphans to a new identity of honesty and adoption into the royal kingdom. God in His love for us has adopted us as sons and daughters through Jesus Christ, to do His will. The spirit of our minds is renewed because we have traded the lies of this world for the truth. Strongholds are broken, thieves steal no more, but use their hands to do good and provide for the needy. Vulgarity, self-deprecation and verbal abuse are reversed to edification, encouragement, comfort, kindness, tenderheartedness and forgiveness. There is unity and maturity because we are emulating our Lord and walking in loving kindness.

Sexual immorality, impurity, greed and decadence is being annihilated. People are no longer drunk with wine, but with the Spirit of God, **Ephesians 5:18.** The light in us is expelling and exposing the darkness, evil and wickedness around us. Every tiny light shining together will create a lighthouse directing the way for the lost to be found. We are making people realize that what we offer is not just confidence tricks, but we are providing them with individual personal benefits for their strength, mutual support, and remedies for grief and bereavement. They can combat feelings of hopelessness and helplessness in times of disaster and conflict and live abundant fulfilled lives with better health and longevity. We are sprinkling a little kindness as confetti wherever we go. It is being received and shining through the windows of the soul and producing a gradual transformation, eventually impacting the universe. Kindness is contagious, when we find simple ways of bringing kindness and joy to others; we bring kindness and joy to the world causing the future generations to thrive and grow. When we lend a helping hand, comfort those who mourn, embrace the neglected, feed the hungry and clothe the naked, we are expressing unconditional love. Unconditional love unites hearts, people, communities and nations who may pay forward what was done to them. It could create a ripple effect touching lives that we may never know. The end thereof we may never see or hear about. This is an example that reveals just that.

The Glass of Milk Story

One day, a poor boy who was selling goods from door to door to pay his way through school, found he had only one dime left, and he was very hungry. He decided he would ask for a meal at the

next house. However, he lost his nerve when a lovely young woman opened the door. Instead of a meal he asked for a drink of water. She thought he looked hungry so she brought him a large glass of milk. He drank it slowly, and then asked, "How much do I owe you?"

"You don't owe me anything," she replied. "Mother taught us not to accept payment for deeds of kindness." He said, "Then I thank you from my heart." As Howard Kelly left that house, he not only felt stronger physically, but his faith in God and man was strong also. He had been ready to give up and quit. Many years later that young woman became critically ill. The local doctors were baffled. They finally sent her to the big city, where they called in specialists to study her rare disease. Dr. Howard Kelly was called in for the consultation. When he heard the name of the town she came from, a strange light filled his eyes. Immediately he arose and went down the hall of the hospital to her room.

Dressed in his doctor's gown he went in to see her. He recognized her at once. He went back to the consultation room determined to do his best to save her life. From that day he gave special attention to the case. After a long struggle, the battle was won. Dr. Kelly requested the business office to pass the final bill to him for approval. He looked at it, then wrote something on the edge and the bill was sent to her room. She feared to open it, for she was sure it would take the rest of her life to pay for it all. Finally, she looked, and something caught her attention on the side of the bill. She read these words....

"Paid in full with one glass of milk"

(Signed)

Dr. Howard Kelly

Tears of joy flooded her eyes as her happy heart prayed:

"Thank You, God, that Your love has spread abroad through human hearts and hands."
– Author Unknown

That story speaks volumes. When something is done without any expectation, there will always be a reward, so go ahead and pay something forward.

KINDNESS

We are becoming a Kingdom Integrated Nation who are Developing Notions for Essential Spirit Saturated citizens."

– Rose Reddy

CHAPTER 15

KINDNESS, A BUILDING BLOCK OF CIVILITY THAT BUILDS HUMANITY

Waht is Civility? Civility is being polite, reasonable and showing respectful behaviour. It is small actions that lead to respect for others and skilfully applied behaviours that lead to positive working relationships and environments. This is an introduction to a culture of KINDNESS, which will open doors of opportunity for the unloved, rejected and abused to be accepted and embraced. When they are engulfed with unconditional (agape, the God kind) love. Stepping out in faith, will birth forth the kindness inside of us; to heal the broken hearts, soften hardened hearts, warm the cockles of cold hearts, change their mind-set and alter their speech patterns. The good person out of the good treasure of the heart produces good, for it is out of the abundance of the heart the mouth speaks, Luke 6:45. We have influence and are delegated to use it for the greater good of others and God's glory. I am not going to be complacent, but am going to get involved, take action, be practical and get dirty in the process, having faith (not religious faith) in my potential to be the hands, feet and voice of God.

I have been re-christened 'Captain Kindness'; and embarked on a journey of awareness, beginning in my Judea (Richards Bay). The first programme was a 30 Day Kindness Challenge, to make teachers and learners aware of the importance of being kind. Examples of acts of kindness were circulated to encourage and educate them, letting them know that it is not an impossible task to accomplish. Teachers participated actively, by encouraging their learners to become involved in the challenge. Despite the offer of prizes being the motivating factor, 450 learners were active contestants.

Participants were rewarded with stickers, badges and gifts for celebrating World Kindness Day at Richards Bay Primary School on 13 November 2020. Bell Equipment, a world leader in the design and manufacture of earth-moving equipment, had partnered with us in creating this kindness awareness. Their BELL helicopter had become synonymous with KINDNESS, by flying to our school with myself as Captain Kindness and Mrs A. du Plessis to award both teachers and learners for their participation.

Richards Bay Primary School

30 Day Kindness Challenge
13 October – 13 November 2020

Smile	Share	Give a flower to someone	Greet	Put a coin in the vending machine
Complement	Open the door for someone	Play with someone new	Make a care package	Encourage someone who is upset
Say something nice to someone	Volunteer	Give to the needy	Say sorry, when you have done wrong	Remember your manners
Say "good job"	Give a hug	Make a get well card	Visit someone who is ill	Take cookies to the old folk
Help carry shopping bags	Write a thank you card to your teacher	Draw a gratitude picture for your parents	Pick up the trash	Take the dog for a walk
Carry your teacher's bag	Let your sibling go first	Decorate the park with kind words on rocks	Say "I love you"	Tidy up without being asked

The learners were overwhelmed by the helicopter landing on our playground, least expecting their two Heads of Department to disembark from it.

They cheered with much excitement, making that the highlight of the day.

Sponsorships from Bell Equipment, Ms Yashika Misree, Jet Chem, family and friends made this event an unforgettable one. Items sponsored by the above were used as token gifts presented to winners and participants of the World Kindness Day activities. Learners, who gave speeches, recited poetry, won colouring-in competitions and wrote poetry were awarded with 'Be Kind' badges and special prizes. Pre-owned toys, clothes and books; were generously sponsored by the learners of Richards Bay Primary School, (RBPS). These were donated to the Richards Bay Family Care, (RBFC) and the Society for the

Richards Bay Family Care

Society for the Prevention of Cruelty to Animals

Prevention of Cruelty to Animals, (SPCA). The event was concluded when everyone present recited this pledge to be kind.

A KINDNESS Pledge

I pledge to myself,

On this very day,

To try to be kind,

In every way.

To every person,

Big or small,

I will help them,

If they fall.

When I love myself, and others too,

That is the best that I can do.

I pledge to be encouraging, supportive, positive, helpful, honest, considerate, thankful, responsible, respectful and a friend.

It was a reminder of the importance of being kind to each other at all times, without the expectation of anything in return.

When our Lord Jesus walked the streets and saw the lepers, he did not spurn them, but touched them with his bare hands and healed them. He was unafraid of being contaminated because He knew the greatness, power and beauty inside each of them was more powerful than the ugliness on the outside. When we embrace those who the world rejects we unearth the hidden beauty, love, joy, kindness, goodness, gentleness and patience that is lying dormant on the inside. The unseen potential is marred under the guise of dirt and degradation and has to be awakened. We are making a contribution to the world, by adding to existing knowledge, without reinventing the wheel, but by adding new features that were not thought about previously. Their identity from useless to useful, ugly to beautiful, worthless to worthy and prodigal children to heirs are changing. It is becoming a reawakening of the dead self to a wonderful resurrected being, who is a partaker of the abundant life promised in John 10:10. God wants to use us as instruments of change, by redirecting people from the broad road that leads to destruction to the narrow road that leads to abundant life. **Romans 12:2 says, "Don't become like the people of this world. Instead, change the way you think. Then you will always be able to determine what God really wants.** How will they change their thought processes? They will look at our lifestyle, which is an example to follow. We

must emulate our Lord Jesus' gentleness of speech, vali-
dating the dregs of society, touching the lepers and forgiving sinners. We will then become role models of excellence to effect change. It is not as the world dictates, but
the expectations of the Lord.

There will be an adjustment of moral, emotional and
spiritual insight and vision. There will be a recovery of
potentials of the human mind as God intended it to be.
The formulas in the brain pertaining to behaviour will
change permanently, instilling kindness, goodness,
tolerance, gentleness and self-control. Their thoughts will
formulate their purpose, which will dictate their actions;
which will become their character, determining their
habits and finally reshaping their life-style. The transformation will solve problems, bring acceptance, peace,
tranquillity, and transformation in and around those who
they interact with. Our actions will include the following:

- To demonstrate love to the unloved.

- To give hope to the hopeless.

- To provide a refuge to the troubled.

- To care for the lost and help them find their way.

- To treat the abused, with compassion.

- To accompany the lonely.

- To uplift those with low self- esteem and give them a
  sense of worth.

- To administer first aid and nurse the sick and feeble.

- To heal the broken-hearted by loving them.
- To rehabilitate the depraved.
- To tend to the neglected and making provision.
- To care for the aged, who are left without family support.
- To favour and support the abused.

Kindness is the basic building block that unites people. It may begin with a warm smile, which is the universal language of love and is highly contagious. You can be the first one to begin the cycle of smiling and watch the magic it creates. A sombre, dull morning will automatically be transmuted into a jovial and blithe day, making it productive.

Kindness in thinking creates perceptiveness, profoundness and discernment in our thought processes, which lead to acuity.

A kind word can bring a smile to one's lips and eyes. The kinder we are, the greater we become. We can change a person who is feeling downcast, by reframing their situation and raising their spirits, just by speaking kindly to them. Timely advice is lovely like golden apples in a silver basket, Proverbs 25:11. Kindness in words creates confidence and opens doors of opportunity for the mute to speak, and share the same joy around. The power of positive affirmations cultivates inner peace, confidence, a sense of worth and confiscates negative comments. A simple compliment will boost egos and make people feel as if the sun is shining down upon them. They would end up being cheerful the entire day, walking with an air of confidence and an inner glowing radiance.

We must surround ourselves with like-minded, happy, generous people, who are ready to give of themselves to benefit others. Remember that words have power to create or kill. It could kill our spirit and belief in ourselves and others. It can shape our lives, by crystallizing perceptions that shape our beliefs, drive our behaviour and eventually create our world. We have to be conscious of what we allow yourselves to listen to, be selective, by keeping the good and discarding the destructive. Words are powerful, they can uplift our being and improve our life or drain us of all our energy. If nobody tells you something kind, motivate yourself, encourage change and boost your self-esteem. Meditate on positive, uplifting thoughts, discard negative words and fill that void with positive self- talk. Speak as you see yourself, not as others do. Call into being that which is not as though it is, Romans 4:17. That will develop an optimistic mind-set. That optimism will reduce negative self-talk, by immediately changing it into positive statements. Be conscious of the words you speak, read and expose yourself to, because of their power. Choose words wisely or they will make us someone we do not want to be. What we listen to will be spoken out of our mouth without any compulsion, embarrassing us in the process.

Kindness in giving leads to gratitude and compassion, which then creates love. It creates a web of improvements around us, by inspiring confidence and enhancing love.

Kindness like love is bestowed as a gift, freely, willingly and without any expectation. Don't be kind to receive kindness, love to be kind. Unexpected kindness is the most powerful. It is the cheapest and most underrated agent of human change. Leo Buscaglia, said; "Too often we underestimate the power of touch, a smile, a kind word, a listening ear, an honest compliment or the smallest act of caring, all of which has the potential to turn a life around. I've learned that you learn best by modelling. If you want people to learn, do it!" Let us heed his sagely advice and become practitioners of kindness.

Actions really do speak louder than words. A civility sanctuary is a practical programme designed and awaiting implementation to transform unacceptable behaviour into acceptable behaviour.

THE CIVILITY SANCTUARY, is a retreat; a place of safety and acceptance where the 'Troubled' can find solace. When the world is against them there is a safe haven they can retreat to. Their inappropriate behaviour either in the classroom or on the playground normally isolates them, but the sanctuary is a place for rehabilitation and reconciliation. In this sanctuary, they will receive individual guidance and rectification of wrong doing. They will receive therapy by embracing them and their challenges with unconditional love. Resources that they were not exposed to will be provided indoors to keep them out of trouble and develop new skills at the various stations with activities. These will be available to draw out the hidden potentials lying dormant within them.

Activities such as playing a musical instrument, doing arts and crafts, learning cultural norms and mores, reading, story writing, chess, drama and indoor games will be taught. They will be purposefully engaged, to develop their potential, and expel disorders. It will be our room of kindness, generosity, tolerance, helpfulness, peace and tranquillity. Each one who enters will promise to try to be: kind, generous, tolerant, helpful and peaceful. They will practise the following:

- To greet when they enter and leave.

- To treat others with kindness.

- To treat others with dignity.

- To show appreciation, by saying thank you.

- To be considerate of those who are slower.

- To wait for their turn.

- Not to push in.

- To smile and not to be angry.

- To use language that is pleasing to all, not foul language.

- To accept those who are not treated well.

- Their habits will change, because habits can be changed in tiny infinitesimal steps. Kindness changes everything.

THE PROGRAMME

In a room that is thematically decorated, the door will be open to receive the kids who the world rejects. The following will be in place to welcome them in.

- Soothing classical or instrumental music will be playing in the background to create an environment of peace and tranquillity.

- Invite them in, they will not be forced to enter.

- Begin with prayer

- Discussion about the misdemeanour ensues, making them feel comfortable.

- The programme will be explained to them, pertaining to their misdemeanour, eg. KINDNESS is not FIGHTING.

- It includes a story or video clips pertaining to fighting.

- After watching or listening a series of questions will be asked, which will cause them to do an introspection of their behaviour.

- A place of admission must be reached, whereby they acknowledge the error of their ways and are prepared to change for the better.

- An alternate activity to replace the fighting will be done.

- A discussion, highlighting the positive action and the attitude or feelings of the recipients.

- Meditate on a proverb or verse to change their thoughts.

- Time of reflection will be done.

Below are some examples of the activities that will be done.

Actions instilled during these activities will be accompanied by a Kindness Card as a reminder of what they have learned. They will be challenged to go out and 'do likewise'. They will be rewarded with special stickers designed for the programme if they are able to complete the challenges and perform those actions. After receiving five of those stickers they will receive a glove embossed with, 'HANDS of ACTION of KINDNESS. This can be worn with pride after performing these acts of kindness. When ten acts of kindness are performed they will be awarded with a Certification of Action and receive another glove of victory.

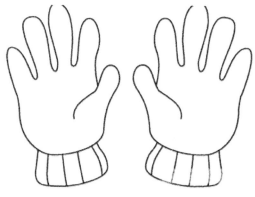

Those become their trophy for each level of achievement. When they have passed ten levels they will receive a final certification of completion and are exempt from the programme. The amazing part of the programme is when the victims of abuse come forth to announce that 'So and So' is being so good in the classroom, on the playground and in the taxi.

ACTIONS and ACTIVITIES

ACTION 1

Kindness is sharing

1 Timothy 6:18, Instruct them to do what is good, to be generous and willing to share.

1. Watch a video clip: Be Kind and Share
2. Have a discussion about the story
3. Role play, by asking them to put themselves into the shoes of those other kids.
4. Ask for examples / activities where sharing can take place.
5. Sing a Sharing song together. "Time to Share"

Colour in a picture.

"Be a little kinder than you have to."
– E. Lockhart

ACTION 2

Patience is waiting without complaining.

1 Corinthians 13:4, Love is patient, love is kind.

1. Watch a video clip: Croc needs to wait
2. Have a discussion about the story.
3. Role play. Ask them to put themselves in the shoes of those kids.
4. Ask for examples / activities where patience takes place.
5. Sing a song together.

"Colour in a picture

Happiness is the new rich. Inner peace is the new success. Health is the new wealth. Kindness is the new COOL.
– Syed Balkhi

ACTION 3

Kindness is not being a bully

1. Watch a video clip: A read along story
2. Have a discussion about the story
3. Role playing- ask them to put themselves in the shoes of those kids.
4. Ask for examples / activities where bullying takes place.
5. Sing a song together.
6. Colour in a picture.

"Change does not roll in on wheels of inevitability, but comes through continuous struggle."
– Martin Luther King Jr.

ACTION 4

Kindness is being tolerant

Ephesians 4:1-2, Walk in a manner worthy of the calling with which you have been called, with all humility and gentleness, with patience, showing tolerance for one another in love.

1. Watch a video clip: Sneeches.

2. Have a discussion about the story.

3. Role play- ask them to put themselves in the shoes of the other kids.

4. Ask for examples of tolerance.

5. Sing a song together.

6. Colour in the pictures

"Kindness in another's trouble,
Courage in your own."
– Adam Lindsay Gordon

"Dare to be different by being KIND,
to yourself and others."
– Rose Reddy

DAILY PROGRAMMES

The programme is designed for defiant children, who cannot help themselves, but get into trouble when left to their own devices during breaks. After a referral to the Sanctuary, parents will be notified about the Programme that their children will be embarking on. Monitors will be selected to assist at the different stations. During breaks they would be welcome to join us where they would be actively engaged. There will be daily activities to occupy them, purposefully.

DAY 1

KIDS FOR CHRIST (K4C)

Volunteers will run the schedule.

1. Sing a few songs
2. Teach a lesson or moral
3. Pray

DAY 2

NATURE'S ENTRY / LANDSERVICE

1. Being an Ambassador for
2. Scientific Experiments
3. Nature lessons and tips
4. Art and Craft activities - RECYCLING

DAY 3
MOVIE DAY
1. Bible story
2. Moral videos
3. Kiddies movies
4. Pop corn

DAY 4
ART & CRAFT ACTIVITIES
1. Painting of a kindness mural
2. Design posters about acceptable behaviour
3. Develop posters/ ideas for notice boards
4. Rock painting with kindness slogans
5. Get well cards
6. Care notes

DAY 5
FITNESS/EXERCISES
1. Zumba- kids online
2. Sport personnel will do an exercise programme
3. Keeping fit also known as Kidd-Gym

When there is kindness, there is goodness.
When there is goodness, there is magic.
Hayley Atwell

FINAL EXPECTED OUTCOMES

When kindness becomes our lifestyle the change effected will be:

- Positive thoughts, feelings and actions will ensue.
- Good relationships will be built.
- Attitudes will be influenced positively.
- Others will be treated fairly, without prejudice.
- Anti-social behaviour and bullying will be reduced.
- There will be an improved sense of acceptance.
- Negative attention seeking will be replaced by acceptance.
- They will be encouraged to do 'nice' things, and be nice to others.
- New values will be learned, especially to those from unsupportive households.
- An innate ability to improve feelings of general well-being will be developed.
- An improved sense of self-esteem and self-confidence will be seen.
- Hearts will melt in the most meaningful ways.
- It will teach us to be content in our everyday life.
- An improved sense of optimism, the opposite of defeatism will be cultivated.
- Improved cognitive development will produce better academic results.
- Kindness will be promoted as a natural and intrinsic way of communication and lifestyle.

- The world will become a better place, by producing confident, caring, resilient, empathetic, and compassionate human beings.

"Tenderness and kindness are not signs of weakness and despair,
but manifestations of strength
and resolution."
– Kahlil Gibran

Be Kind

BIBLICAL EXAMPLES OF KINDNESS

Kindness is not a new concept conceived in the 21st century, but dates back to the beginning of time. These are some acts of kindness that were displayed by men and women of old. We could look at these examples and emulate their actions. Just as they made a difference by their actions, we can also have a great impact on our generation, by keeping the kindness legacy alive.

• Abraham made sacrifices to maintain familial relationships, when he gave his nephew Lot the opportunity to select the best land and relocate. This kindness to Lot, caused God to bless him and his descendants, which is as numerous as the stars in the sky and as the sand on the seashore. It was the induction of God's eternal and glorious covenant with him. He began by changing his name from Abram to Abraham, "exalted father" to "father of a multitude."

- God's kindness is personified in "Jehovah Jireh," our provider, when he provided a ram in the thicket for Abraham to use as a burnt offering instead of his son, Isaac. Abraham was obedient to the call of God to offer his son as the sacrificial lamb. This act is remembered in the New Year prayer. "Remember for us the covenant and loving kindness and oath that You swore to Abraham our father on Mount Moriah, consider the binding with which Abraham our father bound his son Isaac on the altar, suppressing his compassion so as to do Your will, so may Your compassion outweigh Your anger against us." Britannica.com

- Rebekah was a diligent, industrious and sensitive young lady. Her example was in the form of hospitality, when she offered Eliezer, a stranger, a drink and also offered to draw water for his ten camels too. She provided food, straw and lodgings for the night. That act of kindness was gratuitous and rewarded with jewellery and a wedding proposal in **Genesis 24.**

- Joseph was one of 11 brothers born to Jacob, and was despised because he was the favourite. He was beaten, sold to merchants and proclaimed dead to his father, by his brothers. When his brothers went to

Egypt to buy food dur-
ing the famine, Joseph
did not give an eye for an
eye and a tooth for a
tooth; as was dictated by
law at the time. He
instead showed kind-
ness, by feeding them,
making provision for

them, forgiving them and reconciling the family.
There was no act of vengeance or vindictiveness, but
on the contrary, Joseph was affectionate and merciful. He knew that what the devil, through his bothers
intended for evil, God used for good. (Genesis 50:20)

- Pharaoh's daughter showed kindness to a Hebrew
  child and preserved a nation when she had compassion on a baby who was floating down the river. She
  even paid a wage to Jochebed, his mum, to nurse
  him. She later raised him as her son and named him
  Moses. Her act of kindness went against her father's

command that all male
children be killed at birth.
Her act of kindness had
long term significance in
redeeming the Hebrew
slaves from bondage in
Egypt to the Promised
Land.

- God is a God of promise. He is not a man who lies. He made a healing covenant to keep His people free from sickness and disease. The covenant was made certain by joining together God's name and the promise of 'Jehovah-Rapha.' The God who heals. His name declares His nature, as the Healer. His thoughts towards us are about our welfare and health. God revealed Himself as the Healer to the Israelites after their exodus from Egypt.

- When the Israelites had travelled to the Wilderness of Sin they complained to Moses and Aaron. They were hungry and wanted meat and bread. God showed mercy on them and rained bread from heaven in the morning and meat at night. God provided quails for supper and manna for breakfast. There was a miraculous provision for forty years.

- God had called us to wisdom; the fear of the Lord is the beginning of wisdom. Divine wisdom enables us to live civilly, and experience a full and vibrant life. The key to a prosperous life was given to mankind; inscribed by the finger of God, on the tablets of stone that Moses brought down from Mount Sinai. He gave the Israelites the Ten Commandments explained in Exodus 20, which authorises that parents be honoured and respected. We should delight in people, not murder. Treat people with respect, not take advantage of them, by committing fornication and adultery. We should not steal, but ask and we will receive.

- We have to speak the truth at all times, not give false testimony. We should not yearn for things that belong to others. Doing good to others was the governing principle.

- Moral and ceremonial principles taught in the Book of Exodus are a foreshadow of kindness. Men had to respect women and not entice them, but had to marry them. Strangers were not to be mistreated or oppressed. Widows and orphans were not to be afflicted, but taken care of. Money lent to the poor was not to have interest charged on it.

- Moses displayed kindness when he smote the Egyptian who was beating a Hebrew, endangering his life.

- Considering others before himself was a sure sign of greatness. He was considered the rejected deliverer, who had to flee for his life when his actions were discovered. The kindness attribute that seeks the good of others could not be turned off like a faucet in his exodus to Midian; where he rescued some maidens at a well from shepherds who drove them away. His act of kindness unknowingly acquired him a wife, Zipporah. In his gratitude he named his son Gershom, saying "I have become an alien in a foreign land."

- Ruth, a Moabitess, relinquished her idolatry and believed in the Almighty God of the Judeans. She chose to accompany her mother in law back to Judah leaving behind her family and their god. That sacrifice was the greatest act of kindness towards Naomi who was alone. On the advice of Naomi, Ruth went to glean in the fields of Boaz. He showed kindness by allowing her to glean barley and wheat from his field and later by being her kinsman and marrying her. Their union was a mystical and spiritual one that went beyond cultural and forbidden love between a powerful man and a vulnerable younger woman, resulting in their offspring (Obed), being part of the lineage of our Lord Jesus Christ.

- Esther's humble and courageous submission in denying and risking herself for the Jewish peoples' lives is outstanding. Her self-sacrificial giving for the good of others, caused her to pledge her life with no expectation of grandeur or recognition, but the expectation of execution. She and her handmaids fasted and prayed for three days and then she went to stand before the king. She looked past what was affecting them to fulfil God's purpose. She pushed down her fears and put her life on the line to help others. Hers was the perfect example of the love and outgoing concern that we should be practicing towards others. **Esther 2/3**

- **1 Kings 17:7-16** The widow of Zarephath showed kindness to Elijah. She was poor and needy, but put the needs of the prophet before hers and her sons. She prepared a meal for a hungry servant of God, and found that her supply of oil and flour never ran out. Her act of kindness was returned by a miracle from God.

- **Acts 9:36-42.** Dorcas is a woman who cared for the widows and provided clothes for the poor. She was loved by the people. Her death left a void in the hearts of those who she cared for. The people called for Peter; who raised her from the dead.

- **Acts 4:36.** Barnabas was influential in sharing the gospel. He was delighted to see people exhibit the grace of God in their lives. He exhorted and encouraged people to remain faithful. He was nicknamed "Son of Encouragement," because he was inclined to serve others. His dedication was revealed when he sold a field that he owned and brought the money and put it at the feet of the apostles.

- The Good Samaritan, a man regarded as a foreigner stopped to help a man who was robbed, beaten and left for dead. A priest and a Levite saw him and merely walked by, but he took pity and cared for him

by bandaging his wounds and paying for his stay at the inn until his recovery. This neighbourly behaviour was recorded as the ultimate act of kindness, especially across cultural barriers. It emphasises the need for positive action that is beneficial to others.

ACTS OF KINDNESS PERFORMED BY THE APOSTLES

- **Peter,** the rock- called thus by our Lord for his efforts was the rock on which the church would be built. This taught us to point people to God by our godly lifestyle. We women were taught to win over our spouses to Christianity by our examples, not by adorning ourselves outwardly. Men were to be understanding, give honour, and love their wives if they wanted their prayers to be answered. We are to live God's love in such a way that it permeates the whole family, like leaven which causes the whole loaf of bread to rise. He appeals to us to gird the loins of our minds and be sober, obedient, holy and not to conform to lust and ignorance. He requests that we lay aside all malice, deceit, hypocrisy and envy but love and honour all people. We are admonished to be of one mind, having compassion for one another, love as brothers, tender-hearted and courteous. Not to return evil for evil or reviling for reviling, but instead to bless. We are asked to refrain our tongues from evil, our lips from speaking deceit, turn away from evil and do good. We should seek peace and pursue it, be meek, have a good conscience, be hospitable without grumbling and love one another, for love covers a multitude of sins. Peter exhorts us to grow faithful and add virtue to knowledge, knowledge to self-control, self-control to perseverance, perseverance to godliness, godliness to brotherly kindness and brotherly kindness to love. He healed a man who was lame as an act of kindness at the temple gate called Beautiful, and was also taken to task for it, Acts 3. He was not prepared to give him alms instead he made him mobile and to fend for himself, not to be dependent on anyone.

• **Paul** taught love as the guiding principle in our relationships, with both friends and foes. He advocated certain duties be performed to bring about transformed living. We are to love without hypocrisy and be affectionate and honourable to one another. We are to rejoice in hope, be patient in tribulation and steadfast in prayer. We should practice hospitality which is a fruit of the transformed mind. We have to show interest in others and give ourselves to loving and supporting the needy. We should weep with those who weep and bless those who persecute and curse us. We should not be high minded, but associate with the humble. We are requested to live peaceably with all mankind. He concluded by saying do not overcome evil with evil, but with good. We are taught to put on Christ, who is the ultimate example to emulate. He emphasized a high standard of moral conduct.

• **Matthew,** recorded the Sermon on the Mount, teaching us the following:

To be poor in spirit, to receive the kingdom of heaven.

To mourn, and be comforted.

To be meek, thereby inheriting the earth.

To hunger and thirst for righteousness, because we will be filled.

To be merciful so we shall obtain mercy.

To be pure in heart then we shall see God.

To be peacemakers who will be called sons and daughters of God.

To be persecuted for righteousness' sake because the kingdom of heaven is ours.

To be reviled and persecuted and have all kinds of evil falsely spoken against us for God's sake.

In fulfilling all the above we are asked to rejoice and be exceedingly glad, for our reward is in heaven.

He also reminds us that we are the salt of the earth, and the light of the world;

and should let our light shine before men, that they may see our good works and glorify our Father in heaven. That is a format on how we should live and conduct ourselves under God's reign.

The Parable of the Sower is an allegory of the kingdom of heaven, which teaches us how to respond to the Word of God and grow spiritually.

• "Mark 10:45, For even the Son of Man did not come to be served, but to serve, and give His life a ransom for many." Is set within the context of self-giving love of our Lord Jesus Christ. We are taught that the life of discipleship means emulating our Lord in the paths of misunderstanding, rejection and compassion in helping those in need.

• Luke teaches us the importance of prayer. He does this by emphasising our Lord's prayer life. We are reminded that our Lord who is a deity still has to pray to our Heavenly Father; how much more should we, as mere mortals, need to pray. We are taught to be persistent in our prayers and will achieve the expected end through the Holy Spirit, who will empower our prayers.

In the Book of "**Acts 1:8, You shall receive power when the Holy Spirit shall come upon you; and you shall be witnesses to Me in Jerusalem, and in all Judea and Samaria, and to the end of the earth.**"

We are reminded of the empowering of the Holy Spirit in our lives for ministry. We are taught how to live together in meaningful fellowship, sharing freely with one another. He encourages us to be like the people of old, who were ordinary people, who did extraordinary things by faith.

• John confronts us to always have a personal positive response of faith in Jesus Christ and to have life and live it more abundantly. We are taught that life presents us with three tests that we need to pass. These are the test of belief, the test of obedience and the test of love. Our lives have to be characterised by correct belief, godly obedience and brotherly love. He encourages us to love one another and to continue to show hospitality by opening our homes to the needy and providing for those who are labouring in the mission field. We are to live as a family united by bonds of love and generosity, without selfish ambition and jealousy.

Kindness means bearing one another's burdens. We, who are strong, should bear with the scruples of the weak. We ought to edify, be patient and comfort those who are hurting. We are expected to grow in godliness and grace. Love, humility, unity and kindness should motivate our godly living.

ACTS OF KINDNESS PERFORMED BY OUR LORD JESUS CHRIST

There is no one kinder than our Lord Jesus Christ. The kindness that He showed is beyond comprehension. He showed compassion to the prostitutes, the lepers, the blind, the lame, the marginalized, the epileptic, the demon-possessed the dead and the Gentiles. His actions reveal that there is no end to kindness; it can be given to everyone, everywhere and at any time. He taught by leading by example. His acts of kindness are as follows:

• Healing of the leper at the mountainside, who asked Him to make him clean. He looked beyond their physical circumstances of being isolated, untouchable, contagious and dreadful. He reached out and touched the lepers, healing them. Jesus taught us to go beyond social stereotypes, look at where people are coming from, understand their circumstances and develop genuine compassion, manifesting in acts of kindness. We are to learn to love people not judge them.

• Jesus had dinner with Zacchaeus, the tax collector who was also a criminal; who lined his pocket with peoples' hard-earned money. He was frowned upon by society for being a guest of a sinner, but He didn't let the opinion of man dissuade Him. That appointment with Zacchaeus changed his life, causing him to pay back to everyone who he had robbed. He even gave half of his possessions to the poor and paid back four times more of what he had cheated. Society had benefitted from his salvation through one act of kindness. We should not judge people for their wrong doings, but try and right the wrongs done and turn their lives around.

• Our Lord preached to the Gentiles and the Samaritan woman at the well. He did not look at the difference in the creed and cultures, but saw the potential of many lives being redeemed through His tolerance of them. Xenophobia is not only present in today's society, but was prevalent at the time of our Lord as well. He went beyond the prejudice of foreigners, being a Jew, He spoke to a Gentile. By speaking to her He broke all societal boundaries and barriers and showed that kindness is universal. A simple request for water from her, brought about life-changing results. She became the first female evangelist to spread the gospel of our Lord. His actions reveal that kindness should not only be exhibited to our own race; everyone deserves compassion regardless of their skin colour or religious beliefs.

• The woman who had the issue of blood for twelve years, touched the hem of the Lord's garment and was made well. She was not reprimanded for touching Him (she was considered unclean), He instead called her daughter, a term of endearment and told her that her faith had made her well. In breaking the rules of society, her fears turned into ecstasy when she received her healing. Jesus showed her kindness and compassion instead of reproach and rejection. That simple act of kindness sent out a message of acceptance and healing despite gender and societal rules.

• Jairus sought the Lord and begged him to heal his daughter, but on His Way He was stopped by a throng of people and a woman with an issue of blood received her healing. This process delayed our Lord, and He got news that the girl had died. He told the dad not to be afraid, but believe. When they reached the home, Jesus went in with the parents and raised the girl from the dead. It is a powerful story that fills us with hope in every dead situation in our lives. This is proof that God can still step in and perform miracles when we think that all is lost.

• A woman who was caught in adultery was brought to the Lord to stone her as was the law of the day. It was done to test the Lord, who stooped down and wrote on the ground with His finger as though He didn't hear them. After repeatedly being asked he responded by saying, "He who is without sin cast the first stone." Each one was convicted by their conscience and walked away leaving the accused woman by herself. He looked up and asked her where were her accusers and did no one condemn her? Her response was that no one had condemned her. He replied: Neither do I, go and sin no more. The lesson learned from that event is judge not lest we be judged. It is a reminder that God's grace is not a license to go on sinning. When we confess our sins God is faithful to forgive us and cleanse us from all unrighteousness.

• Jesus heals blind Bartemeaus who persisted despite hindrances and rebukes from the disciples who demanded that he be silent. His eyesight was not the only thing that was restored, but his dignity and social standing in the community as well. There was a complete transformation, no longer a beggar dependent on the community for sustenance, but one who could fend for himself. The physical tossing of his cloak was a sign of the change of his status, causing him to belong in society.

• Jesus saw a man lame for 38 years, seated at the Sheep Gate of Bethesda waiting for the waters to be stirred by an angel. The first person to enter the water would be healed of their sicknesses. He asked him if he desired to be made well. He didn't answer with a resounding yes, but complained about others getting in before him. Jesus responded by ordering him to pick up his bed and walk, which he did; because he was immediately healed. He was cautioned to go and sin no more, lest something worse should happen.

- A dad brought his epileptic son to our Lord to be healed. The spirit within the lad caused him to convulse, fall into the fire and water, and threw him on the ground, foaming at the mouth and grinding his teeth. He asked our Lord to have pity on them and to help them. The healing of the boy was questioned by the disciples because they had tried to heal him but failed. The Lord answered and said, "Some things only come out through fasting and prayer."

- Our Lord Jesus cast out a demon that caused destructive behaviour and separated the lad from normal life. He was then accused of doing so by the power of Beelzebub, the prince of demons. When the mute spirit was cast out, the boy began to speak. Our Lord told them that after the evil spirit was expelled, it had to be replaced by the Spirit of God. If not, then that empty space would be reoccupied by evil spirits seeking occupation.

- There is no limit to divine mercy, compassion and kindness. This is revealed in the resurrection of Lazarus from the dead, 4 days later. When all hope was lost, the Lord arrived to call Lazarus forth from the tomb. It is considered the most remarkable miracle performed by our Lord, because it doesn't only reveal his divine power, but His humanity. He loved Lazarus and his sisters, that at the news of his death he wept.

- He reattached the soldier's ear which Peter sliced it off with his spear in defence of the Lord. While hanging on the cross, He asked God to forgive the people who hurt Him. Our Lord also forgave Judas who betrayed Him and the two malefactors who hung on either side of Him on the cross For-  giveness is a great act of kindness that removes guilt from our accusers and ourselves. It gives our enemies a chance to redeem themselves and us an opportunity to heal. He showed the ultimate act of kindness by giving us the gift of eternal life by dying on the cross for our sins.

• Our Lord Jesus Christ was the greatest teacher of all times, who told parables to his disciples to teach them earthly stories with heavenly meanings. These stories are lessons that we and the generations to come can learn from. He did not only teach about things, but did them. He led by example, expecting us to emulate Him. His actions taught us Christian values, such as kindness, compassion, humility, patience, tolerance, gentleness, goodness, and self-  control. He taught us to be led by Holy Spirit educator.

Our Lord's loving-kindness calms the storms in our lives when we feel as if the bottom has fallen out of our world and all is lost. He holds us in an unyielding grip bridging the chasms of hopelessness. When we are lost like the sheep, he will step through the curtain of eternity to find us and return us to safety and the security of his embrace.

ACTS OF KINDNESS PERFORMED TO OUR LORD JESUS CHRIST

Our Lord did not only perform acts of kindness through His miraculous touch, but was also the recipient of acts of kindness.

● **John the Baptist** was the voice crying out in the wilderness. He was the vanguard, who went ahead preparing the way for the Lord, by preaching repentance and baptizing. After the baptism of our Lord by him, He began His ministry.

● **Mark 14:3-9**, While our Lord was a guest in the home of Simon the leper, a woman entered with a vial (alabaster jar) of very expensive and precious perfume of pure nard. She broke the jar, which was the most valuable thing to her and poured the perfume over his head anointing Him. She washed his feet with her tears and dried them with

Those who have been forgiven much, love much.

her hair. She was admonished for her actions; being told that the perfume could have been sold and the money given to the poor.

The Lord's response was, "She has done a beautiful thing to me. The poor you will always have, but you will not always have me." Her actions were not only an anointing of the Lord's body in preparation of his death and burial, but the most compassionate act of lovingkindness. That was a testament of her great love, sacrifice and service that we can take a tip from today to honour our Lord Jesus Christ.

• **Mark 15:43-46**. Joseph of Arimethea risked losing his life, his family, his friends, his status and his religion when he showed kindness and love to our Lord by taking His body and laying it to rest in his tomb. Although our Lord and Saviour was crucified as a common criminal, he dignified His death, by giving Him the burial of a king, in an unused tomb. His loving kindness towards Jesus revealed the true power of the resurrection.

"If you see someone without a smile,
give them one of yours."

– Dolly Parton

OUR PURPOSE IN LIFE

When God speaks promises we need to respond in optimism, despite the time delay. In the fullness of time God will manifest His promises. As ambassadors of the Kingdom, we represent kingdom matters and policies. We help to promote peace, kindness, love, tolerance and charity. As representatives of the Lord we have to maintain positive relationships with the people who we interact with. Our personality has to be distinctive enough to separate us from the crowd. We should be creative, intuitive, sensitive, original, nonconforming innovative, confident, optimistic, compassionate and empathetic. We have to direct people from pessimism to optimism and not become weary in doing well. It is human nature to get tired, but when it comes to showing kindness or doing good to one another, we should not. When we do get weary of showing kindness, meanness will set in and we will begin to hate and backbite one another; becoming desensitised. That will tarnish the fabric of Christianity and friendship. We will also lose the reward that God has prepared for us. Let us lead by example and leave a legacy of kindness, wherever we go. Others must be able to tread in our footsteps when we have left the earth to make an impression for others to follow. Kindness has a connotation of weakness and naiveté, but that is not so; it requires courage, strength and skill. Science has found that devoting our time, talent and treasures to others brings everlasting well-being, satisfaction and stability.

We are commanded to give to the one who begs, and not to refuse the one who would borrow from us.

If anyone would sue us and take our tunic, we should let them have our cloak as well. When we are forced to go one mile, we should go two miles. It has been said that, "We should love our neighbour and hate our enemy," but we should love our enemies, do good to those who hate us, bless those who curse us and pray for those who persecute us. We are called to freedom, not using it as an opportunity for the flesh, but to serve one another with love and kindness.

Kind words which are beneficial to gladden heavy hearts and raise the spirit of the down-trodden should be used. Let us eradicate anxiety, which demoralizes and create doubts in the minds of people who we interact with, by being positive, compassionate and tolerant.

Acts of kindness are simple, free, positive and healthy. Kindness is good for the body, mind and spirit. It increases self-esteem, improves the mood and sense of connectivity with others. It eliminates loneliness, and enhances relationships because it is contagious. This positivity is like planting seeds of kindness in the garden of our minds and watching it grow. Our kindness, tolerance and patience leads to repentance and other acts of kindness being perpetuated. If kindness and truth are bound around our necks and written on the tablets of our hearts, then we will win favour and a good name in both God's and man's sight.

We have been chosen of God, as holy and beloved, so let us put on a heart of compassion, kindness, humility, gentleness and patience, to do justice and to walk circumspectly with Him and man. We're reminded to show hospitality to strangers, be devoted to one another and not give preference to one another; for every simple act of kindness changes the universe.

We may not always be appreciated when we are nice to people, but we will surely be when we show kindness.

We can only be cool until we are thirty years old, but we can be kind for our whole life. Be a kind friend, because that is the right kind of friend. If we do our little bit of kindness wherever we go, all put together will overwhelm the world. It affects the giver and the recipient, by leaving an impression on both.

In this fast paced world kindness is taking a back seat to selfies, self- interest and expendable human interactions. What we need desperately are peacemakers, healers, and lovers of kindness. We need people of moral courage, who are willing to make this world humane. Kindness is fundamental to the human existence. We are enriched with kindness from our nurturing parents. We are wired for kindness; it is sewn into the framework of our DNA. It does not demand hard work, but originates from simple acts of doing no harm to others. Kindness bites the tongue that wants to retaliate to preserve peace of mind.

Kindness broadens our life's frame of reference and is a symbol of respect and value to the receiver. It should be a competition in which we all strive for first place but everyone wins. The beauty of kindness is that it is open to anyone. We can all opt to choose it, because it is freely accessible and universally understood. When practised it sends out ripple effects of well-being through society. It is socially transformative when it is paid forward.

We are commissioned to feed the hungry, quench the thirst of the thirsty, be hospitable to strangers, clothe the naked, provide care to the sick and visit prisoners who are held captivate in their mind and body. The first three are duties that we should duly perform, humanity dictates that we relieve our worst enemies when they are perishing from hunger and thirst, by providing them with food, water and hospitality. The next three are voluntary acts of self-forgetting love.

Clothing the naked indicates a liberal and loving spirit, visiting the sick is an act of spontaneous self-sacrifice and visiting the outcasts in prison is an act of charity

In **Matthew 25:40,** the Lord said, **"Whatever you do for the least of these brothers and sisters of mine, you did unto me."** God wants our lives to overflow with mercy, love, compassion and kindness. Our generous actions will reduce poverty and save lives. We can extract the less fortunate and abused from starvation, nakedness, homelessness, violence and exploitation. Lives will be restored, the pariahs will feel dignified and communities will be empowered. Their passions, drive and talents will be unleashed. They inevitably break the cycle of poverty and lack; are able to take responsibility, make money and finally give back to the community that redeemed them. By doing the above we will be serving the poor and oppressed emulating our Lord's action. Lives will be transformed, because our Lord Jesus Christ is the Bread of life; who will sustain them today and equip them to put bread and food on their tables tomorrow. Water is essential to life; Jesus is the source of Living Water, who will quench the physical and spiritual thirst; making them thirst no more. Providing a safe refuge for strangers, will show them that they are not left unnoticed and forgotten; but are our neighbours. Instructing the ignorant, alarming the careless, encouraging the desolate, comforting the distressed, strengthening the weak, confirming the wavering, reclaiming the wicked and edifying the righteous are acts of spiritual mercy; kindness. We should clothe ourselves with these garments as part of our daily apparel. In our conduct we should be recognized as imitators of the kindness and benevolence of God the Father.

"Constant kindness can accomplish much.
As the sun makes ice melt,
kindness causes misunderstanding,
mistrust and hostility to evaporate."
– Albert Schweitzer

CHAPTER 17

FORGIVENESS IS KINDNESS MANIFESTED

Be kind to one another, tender hearted, forgiving one another,
as God in Christ forgave you,

– Ephesians 4:32

What is forgiveness?

Forgiveness is pardoning an offender. Biblically, it means "to let go," especially of debt. Luke 11:4. It is about goodness and extending mercy to those who harmed us. It is the act of deciding to live with the painful consequences of other peoples' malicious actions, without bitterness, rancour and hatred. If we do, our souls are threatened to

> Everyone makes mistakes. If you can't forgive others, don't expect others to forgive you.

be destroyed. It is strong medicine for emotional wounds. When life hits us hard there is nothing more effective than forgiveness for healing those deep wounds.

Acts of kindness to bring about forgiveness

We can begin doing simple acts of kindness, such as greeting warmly, providing a meal for the sick, taking in the dustbin after it has been emptied. The last thing that they expect is sustained kindness and strength. When evil meets with goodness it will be disarmed and stunned into incredulity. The offender will be compelled to look inward, and do good. Kindness breaks the enemy's spell and renders him powerless. Our light of kindness will shine in the face of darkness, expelling it and melting hardened hearts. Forgiveness will pursue relationships, bring about restoration and the will to love again.

Why should we forgive?

- It brings healing and closure.

- To help increase self-esteem and give inner strength and safety.

- It reverses lies, such as "I am not worthy, I am defeated."

- It allows us to move on in life with meaning and purpose.

- It produces strong psychological benefits, such as decreasing depression, anxiety, anger and post-traumatic stress disorder.

There is no love without forgiveness, and there is no forgiveness without love.

The forgiveness process?

- One little bit at a time.

- Show love in small ways every day.

- Do whatever we can to be at peace with one another.

- Show compassion in the face of wickedness.

- Extend care when we are harmed.

- Begin by making a commitment not to retaliate.

- Remember that we are all unique, special and irre-placeable.

- Cultivate a mind-set of valuing humanity.

- It is not condoning the wrong act; it is simply letting go.

- Be empathetic, we all have imperfections and would love to be forgiven, likewise we should forgive too.

- We should be reasonable and tolerant to put up with minor misdemeanours.

- We must act quickly to forgive before it lingers and festers into bitterness.

- Reconciliation and restoration of lost relationships through admitting that we are at fault and are sorry.

- Trust, confidence and delight is a new journey that is not reached overnight, but over time.

- Forgiveness is not forgetfulness, but the knowledge that misdemeanours have been erased.

- Let go of anger and resentment, it will keep us calm,

improve our health and increase our happiness.

- We forgive when we let go of resentment and give up a claim for compensation for any loss.

- Try to reach the stage of unselfish love, which does not keep a record of any wrongdoing.

What is *unforgiveness* and what does it do?

- It is a state of mental distress that results from not accepting the remorse expressed by the offender.

- A feeling of restitution which overwhelms demanding punishment.

- The emotional rollercoaster which controls thoughts, speech and actions.

- We become emotionally and mentally challenged.

The weak can never forgive. Forgiveness is an attribute of the strong.

- Mahatma Gandhi -

- Keeps us imprisoned in our turmoil and pain, ruining relationships, because it is infectious and noxious.

- It prevents one from moving on, holding one hostage, and hampering good relationships.

- It is equated to one carrying a heavy load; the longer one carries it, the heavier it grows.

- It pushes down roots of bitterness, which entangles one deeper into the crucible of toxins.

- It leaves behind emotional wounds of fear, rejection, betrayal and uncertainty.

- Emotional wounds that become infected leads to unforgiveness, antagonism, acrimony, unkindness and despair.

- It breeds stress and produces sickness and disease.

- It is a severe hindrance to prayer.

What does forgiveness do?

- Let us be like our Lord who forgives all our iniquities, and heals all our diseases. He also reminded us to forgive 70 x 7 times a day.

- It helps us to embrace each other and move forward.

- We develop healthier relationships.

- It will remove that mountain that weighs heavy on our hearts.

- Forgiveness and good health are directly proportional; which means forgiveness brings about healing of sickness and diseases.

- There is improved mental health, less stress, anxiety and hostility.

- Our immune system and self-esteem becomes stronger.

"Forgiveness is one of the most powerful gifts you can give yourself."

– Katrina Mayer

MY UNIQUE HEART

CHAPTER 18

When we reminisce, we will be amazed at the kindness that we experienced and how we made others feel. Our little acts of kindness have meant so much to others, that they put a smile in their hearts to see the difference that was made. Our actions and kind words had soothed peoples' hurt, eased their struggles, filled their bellies, warmed their hearts, embraced them when they were rejected and made deposits in their memory banks. On dark and dreary days our acts of kindness can be the sunshine. We can be the rainbow in someone's cloud.

Acts of KINDNESS which has made a difference

When I was a young lady I had inadvertently discovered an illiterate eight-year-old boy. Relatives adopted this little boy who was left homeless, when his parents were imprisoned. He was the offspring of foetal drug and alcohol syndrome, with learning disabilities. By the time he turned eight he was unschooled and just called 'BOY'. He had been sent to school, but was unteachable and was sent back home. After I discovered his history I embarked on teaching him to read and write. He was brought home daily; where he received basic reading and writing lessons. With much persuasion, a little bit of love, attention and life skills the rehabilitation process of a little nameless boy began.

I named him Jairus after the ruler from the Bible who wanted his daughter healed by our Lord Jesus Christ. He accepted his new identity with much delight. Because he sought the transformation, it was easier than anticipated. After a while he acquired the necessary skills and resumed lessons at school and is now a productive citizen.

Candice, was the prettiest girl at school, who had begun school a year before the rest of us. She struggled in grade one and had to repeat the year. She progressed to the next two grades and kept behind in each phase. By the time she got to high school, she had an inferiority complex. She tried to conceal her lack of cognitive skills by focussing on the opposite sex. I convinced her to return home immediately after school and work with me, while my homework was being done. Individual attention in all subjects were offered, which built up her level of expertise and confidence. She began passing tests, excelled in her oral work and came to a realization that she could do all things through Christ who gives her strength. She has finished school, married a Pastor and is busy giving back to the community.

Rayden, a seven-year-old, came to school just to be out of the house and in a safe place, where someone showed interest in him. There were stories about parents being here, there and everywhere, but home to receive, feed and clothe him. He remained at school until I left after all my marking, planning and preparation for the next day was done. While I was busy, he was helped with his homework. He sat quietly in my reading corner and gobbled up all the reading material that was available to him until I was ready to leave. My itinerary included a stop at the local store to purchase bread, milk and make a visit to the public library. During those trips as part of my entourage, were my two daughters and Rayden. He requested that I apply for a library pocket for him so that he could also borrow as many books as was allowed. To my surprise and joy this young lad developed a love for reading. This love and passion for books created a genius in every aspect of the English language and kept a lonely and neglected little boy out of all societal ills. Fortunately, for me, I met this young man 10 years later, and was given the biggest hug from a seventeen-year-old, who proudly reiterated, "Mam, I still love reading."

There were two siblings at my place of worship who were cognitively challenged and struggled tremendously at school. One was in Secondary School, while the younger sibling was in Primary School, but still grappled to read and write. This had a devastating effect on all learning areas. I assisted the older sibling with research material via the internet, printed it and helped with assignments and projects. She also received extra tuition from my older daughter, Trevishka, while I assisted the younger sibling. They read through the material, explained the content and assisted with the completion of all their homework. This continued for an entire year, until their mum was able to afford to buy a computer. We installed it and taught them the basic skills to acquire the necessary information that was required. She became self-reliant and had mastered the skill of research. While she was being taught all the various subjects, her little brother was being taught to read material from a much lower level than his competency. His comprehension and creative writing skills were expanding, while his self-esteem also developed. Over a period of three terms the entire Junior Primary reading scheme was redone under direct supervision. This was done an hour before church on Tuesdays, Wednesdays and Fridays and for two hours on Sunday afternoons. During these 2 hours we recapped the entire week's activities. Time spent on those siblings was not time wasted, but time invested. They are both literate and are no longer statistics of the illiterate of the Outcomes Based Education. Most important, for me they could read their Bibles.

A few years ago I walked into a grade one classroom to find an obese six-year-old with six slices of bread, a packet of chips, a box of juice, a chocolate and a tub of yoghurt packed into her lunch bag. During my interaction with her over the next few days, I discerned that Sarah was a daughter of an absentee mum, who worked abroad to supplement the income and over compensated for her absence by providing for her physical needs. Maslow's hierarchy of needs revealed that her physiological needs, which included food, water, warmth, rest, safety and security were met, but her psychological needs were not. The absence of belonging, love and esteem needs; led to a girl, who ate her way into happiness. In doing so, she isolated herself from everyone else who judged her and she became a recluse. In her solitary state she withdrew into herself and experienced difficulty identifying letters, words and numbers. After talking to both her and the grandparents she was taught proper healthy eating habits. She remained after school for an hour with me, and by the end of the second term she was on par with my best learners. That boosted her self-actualization and she became a top achiever. I was privileged to teach her again two years later in grade three. To my amazement she became a model student, to whom others looked up to. She also made the top ten in the class. When she was in grade seven, had been selected as a prefect and she now oozes confidence.

A young lady from a remote village in Kwa-Zulu Natal moved to Richards Bay ten years ago. She became part of our family through our interaction at church. With much embracing and nurturing she has become accustomed to our way of life and is now an 'adopted spiritual' daughter. During times of difficulty and challenges, she is welcome to come home; knowing that our doors would always be open. She is also an excellent support structure for my girls when they need to give vent to their feelings. I'm honoured to be a mother of another unofficial adopted-daughter. She insinuates that I am a prophetic, inspirational and motivational human being who is also a substitute mother. One from whom I always receive a Mother's Day gift.

Cusak, Lucerne, Prudence, Charlene, Draline, Wesley were but a few youths who walked through our doors due to varying disturbing circumstances, crying out for help and an embrace.

A warm bed, a hot meal and encouraging words have been the catalyst in their lives. They got to look at their parents from a new and different perspective and appreciate their input; whether it was negative or positive. They overcame their suicidal tendencies and now have a positive outlook in life.

The Biblical Counsellor in me seemed to be the antennae that always sought the emotionally needy. My ears listened attentively to the cries of their hearts and out of the abundance of my heart came forth the healing balm of Gilead that brought healing and deliverance. The words of God became the lamp to their feet and a light to their path to redirect them back into the house of God and His word.

At my present place of employment, there are a few Indian employees. Being an offspring of the apartheid era, I grew up with an inferiority complex thinking that 'white people' were better than we are. We were looked down upon as people who were not good enough. When God elevates us to new dimensions, then we are regarded as equals in every arena. I became the School Counsellor who sat in confidence in front of people who disregarded me, but my ability dictated that they open themselves fully. The wisdom of God enabled them to walk out, head held high and a smile on their faces knowing that there is hope in their hopeless situations. Words of kindness are like silver apples in golden baskets, pleasing to the ear and the palate.

Marriages were reconciled under the advice of God and Biblical Counselling. Parental guidance, youth counselling and therapy were provided to people of different races, cultures and creeds. The world is seeking answers

to their questions and solutions to their problems. God's education system has the answers to bring about mediation. When bodies are presented as a living sacrifice to God, they will be transformed by the renewing of their minds. A godly paradigm makes all the difference. It does not happen miraculously overnight, but grows from one stage to the next.

Low self-esteem in adults was eradicated through the word of my testimony and the promises from the Word of God. We had a Prayer Group at school, where we gathered weekly to pray and exhort each other. Through that gathering we had numerous prayers answered. We do not gather anymore due to Covid 19 protocols, but we still pray and encourage each other online. God has been faithful in answering prayers and protecting our school from the ravages of Covid 19. Although the first Covid 19 case reported in Richards Bay was from our school, we can give praise to God that none of our staff or students succumbed to the clutches of Covid 19 in death.

Love is patient, kind. It does not dishonour others and does not keep records of wrongs.

1 Corinthians 13

BECOMING AN AMBASSADOR OF KINDNESS

W hen we challenge ourselves and delve into the intrinsic part of our being, we will be able to cultivate something of understanding, acceptance, tolerance, compassion and greatness. What we find in the innermost part of our hearts will offer assistance, hope and encouragement to countless people who are experiencing the same challenges that we had gone through. That would bring hope for a turnaround in their circumstances. In the uniqueness of our eyes, ears, lips, tongues, teeth, fingers, feet, voice and gait; we have a story to tell, which is just as different as we are. When God created us in His image, (**Genesis 1:27**), He gave us His spiritual, emotional, and intellectual imaging and will. We feel sorrow, joy, anger and fear, because those are our emotions. We make choices by reason and discernment, through our intellect. We are sentient beings, self-aware and self-conscious of who we are. We are aesthetic creatures, therefore we love beautiful things and enjoy the beauty around us. God, after His Creation looked and said, "It is good." Out of that same goodness, let us create something that will add value to what already exists. We have the power of life on our tongues, (**Proverbs 18:22**). We can speak and create with our words, by calling into being that which is not as though it were, (**Romans 4:17**). Let us architect the future, by giving life to the potential that is lying dormant inside of us. We can unlock and maximise the dream seeds inside of us. We should not allow fear and ridicule to stifle those roots and shoots that are breaking through and into the grounds of our being.

The fear that we have, will be turned into faith, when put into the hands of the Almighty God. Faith will lead us to believe that all things are possible, **Matthew 19:26.**

Those nuggets inside of us, will become the catalyst, to bring about change in activities, events and lives that will be noticeable. Through our speech, enthusiasm and energy, we could cause others to become friendly, enthusiastic and more energetic. Those who are depressed, closeted indoors; afraid to come out into society, for fear of rejection, being ostracised, belittled and gossiped about; will feel a sense of warmth in their hearts and defy societies prejudices and step out with pride and joy.

Smiles will warm their lips and a radiant glow will brighten their countenances.

By revealing to the world what is inside of us, we will be making a contribution of adding value to their existing knowledge. Our passion and desire to see change in others will become a movement for improvement. It can be ACTION personified. It can become a practical, everyday tool for a change in the direction that their lives should take. We will make history with our stories of hope. Problems of humanity will be solved with our godly solutions. **God has given us the keys to the kingdom. (Matthew 16:19)**, You will have complete and free access to God's kingdom, keys to open any and every door: no more barriers between heaven and earth. Those

same keys can also be used to shut the doors of sickness, death, disappointment and devastation in our lives. We will be redefining education, society and the world in a way that makes life work in real time. Holy Spirit, our Educator will teach us all things and direct our footsteps, because **the footsteps of the righteous are ordered by God, Psalm 37:23.** He will help us discover and create new information which cannot be researched, find new learning systems and methodology; which will turn the world system around. Income producing ideas will exhibit the entrepreneur in us, creating an excellent chance of embracing and understanding the needs of the time. We will create products and systems that we could use to improve, to simplify life and change society.

We will become a link in the chain to create God's masterpiece for this and the coming generations. Let us become the people who are acknowledged for opening our mouths with words of wisdom and the teaching of kindness on our tongues. Let us extend our hands towards the poor and the needy. If we have two coats, we should give one away. We should share our food with those who do not have it. John the Baptist told the tax collectors who extorted money, not to, but to take only what is required by law; we should do likewise. He told the soldiers to be content with their rations, not to shakedown and blackmail. Those of us in similar positions should not take advantage of our stature and mistreat people under our authority.

BECOMING PRACTITIONERS OF KINDNESS

When we look around us and see the devastation and chaos caused in this world? We cannot stand by and watch, without doing anything to bring about change. Our incremental ideas will eventually display the drastic change generated. Let us be the first to act, and slow to speak.

Children are the victims of our sick and debauched society. Absentee parents are not providing the basic needs, such as food, clothing, love, protection and safety. These children grow up uncultured, unloved, unprotected and open to the evil around them and the fears in their head. Multiple parenting, through divorce and cohabitation, has produced a generation of misfits with inferiority complexes. These square bodies are tirelessly trying to squeeze themselves into round holes, with no success. They are wreaking havoc wherever they go in search of love, acceptance and attention.

Parents, grand-parents, teachers, care-givers, day-care and after-care centres, who watch over children daily are posed with undisciplined, non-submissive children with a blatant disregard for authority. Instant gratification is demanded by these children; guilty parents yield to their demands to pacify them. Do we want to be martyrs and right the wrongs of society? Do we want normal children; not ones who are pumped with medication to fit into society? Do we want to see zombies, returning to active, energised, living beings who can fit into society and become productive? If we are passionate to see change in what the world is accepting as the norm, then we are the best candidates to begin the implementation process.

We can begin with one individual at a time; who can set the standard for who they should grow into by removing and replacing their evil nature to one that is good, kind, gentle, peaceful, tolerant and meek. Remember that this is not a process that can be rushed into, but with much patience and tolerance, they have to be guided and only then will we see the benefits of our sowing. We can teach them to forgive, release hurt and learn to walk in love, thereby seeing themselves as we do, profitable members of society. We can remove the state of dis-ease, which inevitably results in sickness and disease of the body, mind and spirit. Diseases of the mind, lead to warped thought processes which lead to perversion and undesirable behaviour such as sexual abuse and molestation. We are the way we think, when those thought patterns are changed, then we become new people. Diseases of the body are sometimes self-inflicted, psychosomatic and through lack of proper nourishment. By providing nourishment to the body, we create a healthy body, which is filled with pride, self-esteem and confidence. Sickness vanishes when bodies have sustenance. Disease of the spirit results from being unloved, rejected, fearful, neglected, condemned and separated.

We have the keys to provide an open door of acceptance, assurance, love, commendation and inclusivity. Our embrace may be the only welcome and support that they have ever received, so let us stretch out our arms to encompass them. A friendly demeanour, a warm smile and a simple greeting is the pathway to acceptance.

We must find every opportunity to initiate a difference in our society. At social gatherings and seminars where awareness, remediation measures and issues are discussed we must relate our experiences with defiant children and discuss the steps implemented to bring about change in their behaviour. That would motivate the audience enough to want to execute the programme, to create change in their homes, families, classrooms, schools, communities and society at large. Questions about specific behavioural patterns will be answered with examples from our experience. If we do not have answers to questions, because of our lack of knowledge or experience, then we will be charged to find solutions for those incidents. It can later be added as innovative addendums to the programme.

We may not have all the answers to every question, but we can find them, when we search within. We can introduce pilot programmes to various audiences, who deal with children. We can do follow-up sessions at those centres and video record their progress. We should interview personnel who have implemented the programme, to ascertain the successes and failures encountered. When the successes outweigh the failures, they can then be integrated as part of their activities to effect change. The situations that these children are in can be used to change them because we cannot always change their circumstances. Volunteering to help will remove criticism and expulsion and bring about acceptance for change.

Promote the programme by teaching it to parents, church leaders, community workers, teachers and Early Childhood Development Associations by holding workshops. Detailed explanations pertaining to the programme can be discussed. Role playing can be done with the candidates attending the workshops. Provide them with the beginning of the programme to rouse their interest to want to acquire the complete programme.

Empower the underprivileged by sponsoring copies of the programme, especially to the rural areas where there is a struggle with discipline, mentorship and management of children who do not have parental guidance. These mentors will manage the insanity and coordinate the chaos, by being there and dealing with the emotional outbursts. When we avail ourselves to be present and engaging then anger, hostility and boredom will be reduced. A new sense of responsibility will arise, causing them not to be indifferent any longer, but to become conspicuous in their behaviour and academics.

Others can be inspired by our actions in making a difference in the lives of children who they have given up hope in. When our loving kindness is extended and endured, fear will be replaced with trust. It will make a difference in them, affirming their value and worth. They will learn that they are not perfect, just forgiven and will be loved unconditionally. Those broken vessels will be in the hand of a potter, who will help to remould and reshape them into vessels of honour. They will not only be made new, but they will be free from themselves. Guilt can no longer hold them down as victims, they will arise triumphantly.

When testimonies of success stories are shared; people would be motivated to become guinea pigs, as long as there is a difference in the final outcome. Names and places will be changed to conceal the identity of the successful.

All the Social Media platforms can be utilized. These messages can be communicated at gatherings where both adults and children are present, at parent meetings and at youth meetings where unruly behaviour is witnessed. The programme can be used as a replacement of medication to control impulsive behaviour. Practice, practice, practice makes perfect. We have to live the life that others would want to emulate. Reverse psychology will guarantee a change in attitude, towards themselves, peers, siblings, parents and teachers. Respect will become vocal and demonstrative. Just as the light that blinded Saul on his way to Tarsus, also opened the heart of an Apostle. Social and emotional learning will take place in individuals. Negativism will be substituted with positive reinforcement and affirmations. **"Let the righteous strike (correct) me — it is a kindness [done to encourage my spiritual maturity]. It is [the choicest anointing] oil on the head." Psalm 141:5.**

We can become ambassadors of kindness, by clothing ourselves with kindness, Colossians 3:12, and garments of righteousness. It is something that touches hearts and changes lives deeply. Kindness empowers others to be the difference and speaks volumes to those who receive it.

"Unexpected kindness is the most powerful, least costly; and most underrated agent of human change."

Bob Kerrey

World Kindness Day 2020

BECOMING THE PROVERBS 31 PERSON

- Proverbs 31 provides us with invaluable insight on what a godly person should look like. These are attributes to live by and impart to people who we will interact with. We have to live our entire lives out of a desire to honour and serve the Lord, only then will we become virtuous people.

- We can begin by teaching people not to drink and forget their poverty and remember their misery no more, because it will bring destruction.

- Beer and wine should not be craved, because they will forget what was decreed and deprive the oppressed of their rights.

- Remind them that beer is for those who are perishing and wine is for those who are in anguish and only brings temporary relief.

- Be the mouthpiece of those who cannot speak for themselves, upholding and defending the rights of the destitute.

- Focus on what is the truth and not what the world dictates.

- Be strong, wise, conscientious, loving, caring, hard-working and faithful.

- Endeavour to do good not harm.

- Eat not the bread of idleness, but be industrious people.

- Be shrewd business people, enterprising traders, generous benefactors and wise teachers.

- Do not only impact others, but motivate them to emulate our actions.

- Let our outward actions be an indication of the virtue inside our hearts.

- Let others use our works as a plumb-line of our worth.

We can become modern Proverbs 31 people in this corrupt world, by becoming super heroes who are constantly, loving and taking care of our families and juggling things with poise and grace; without capes. We can be trustworthy, encouraging and comforting to those around us. In our wisdom, we can empower others spiritually, mentally and physically to accomplish their God-given assignments. Our generous nature will allow us to share our abundance or lack of food, clothing, money, time and talent. We can use our material resources to train and mentor the human resources that we have at our disposal, making them skilled leaders. Let us live with purpose, diligence, forgiveness and repentance. Use the intelligence that we have to make things, be a wonderful homemaker, who is praised by our spouses, adored by our children, and take care of the physical needs of others; not only our families. Let us be in shape, physically, mentally, emotionally and; so that we can speak words of wisdom to help others.

OUR HOME -
A KINDNESS SANCTUARY

My childhood home and my home since my marriage, has been a safe haven to the lost, sick, weary, suicidal, hopeless, financially challenged and missionaries.

It has been a hospital for the sick to be treated and healed. A recuperation centre for those in recovery. Weak and weary bodies were bathed, moisturised, fed and clothed. Medical assistance was provided to those who did not have the means. Massages, reflexology and most importantly prayers were the treatment provided to them.

It has been the counselling centre for those requiring therapy and rehabilitation. Friends and family sought counsel when they were confused, disturbed and perplexed. Their confusion was transformed into clarity, their disturbances into stability and their perplexity into enlightenment. Marriages that were falling apart at the seams were sewn together with chords of love through repeated counselling and care. Temporary separations made the hearts grow fonder and relished the lost love. Forgiveness was the glue that bound couples together, by relinquishing the past mistakes and looking to God as the author and perfecter of our faith.

It has been a school-house for those requiring remediation with academics, beginning with children as old as three years-old to adults who were studying at tertiary institutions. Tuition was provided at no cost to students. They were even transported to their homes late in the evenings. People have walked through the doors seeking succour and left satisfied and confident. Material resources were provided to students. Our home was the go-to place when things were not okay. Family politics drove many youths away from their homes as runaways contemplating suicide.

The look of disillusionment on my girls' faces spoke volumes, when they encountered such situations at school or university. "Mum, so and so is in trouble." We got into my car and fetched these troubled souls. A warm embrace, a meal and a bed to lay their confused head was the initial provision. Thereafter, Biblical counsel was provided depicting the pros and cons of their actions; making them realise the futility of their actions and returning them back to relieved and grateful parents.

During my service as an educator, I came across many teachers who were appointed to different provinces and who had no accommo-dation. They found a safe harbour at our home until they were proficient enough to fend for themselves. One such person was a blessing to me during childbirth, when my husband had a broken femur. I believe that she was an angel sent in disguise to assist me when my husband was out of commission. She resided with us for two years until she got married.

Many who lost their way, found our home as a place of refuge to return them back to God. Our home was a church for those needing prayer and deliverance. Hours were spent in counselling and prayer. When I became weary in my humanness and looked at my limited abili-ties; I sought the assistance of my spiritual parents, who were ever ready to assist. They responded immediately after telephone calls were made to exorcise demonic spirits and to counsel further. Those empty spiritual domains had to be cleaned and filled with the spirit of God, through Bible studies and prayer.

The old, ashamed and rejected came and found a sense of worth, care and belonging with us. We pampered them, by tinting and straightening their hair, painting their nails, giving them head and back massages. We helped people regain their dignity by plucking out the old deformed feathers and awaited the growth of new ones, like that of the eagles. Those who had made poor financial decisions were advised and assisted until they were financially stable. Our life's lessons were taught to them, assuring them that there is hope in the future as long as we have our eyes focused on our Father in heaven, who is our provider.

Spiritual, physical, mental and emotional healing has been ministered at our refuge. The troubled, tearful and tired found rest for their weary souls, and returned happy and restored back to their families. Food, clothing and finances were provided to those who had none. They were transported to work and school daily until they could provide for themselves. Worrywarts who were troubled by mental and emotional anguish were prayed with and taught to leave their burdens at the feet of our Lord. Spiritual upliftment came from studying the Word of God, which is bread for our spiritual nourishment.

The unemployed were empowered by being employed at my husband's business. After his retirement due to loss of his sight through glaucoma, he set up his employees to take over his clientele and continue with the business.

Our gardener of many years was also gainfully employed by a major company, expanding his skill set and increasing his self-worth.

Many work colleagues, who experienced difficulties at their old schools were employed at new schools through my introductions.   Under my mentorship they have adapted to the differentiated teaching methodology and different races. They have become permanent employees of the state and are satisfied and successful at what they're presently doing.

Housewives who were content caring for their spouses and children were motivated to study and are now qualified teachers, masseuses, and gainfully employed.

Many missionaries of different races, who had visited South Africa had experienced our hospitality, because the church was unable to provide accommodation. We drove them to and from venues where meetings were held. We sacrificed our bedroom for them to lay their heads. While lying on our pillows they prayed for the salvation of my then unsaved husband. Godly advice, encouragement, inspiration and prayer are the pillars that people lean on when they enter our home. The presence of God permeates our peaceful and safe haven, allowing people to spew out their troubles and be replenished with the powerful presence of God. The anointing received had broken bondages and set the captive free from sin and degradation.

PRAYER THE ULTIMATE ACT OF KINDNESS

Prayer is equivalent to supplying a need or performing routine maintenance. It is a form of service rendered. It is how we help repair an emotional wound. It is the best prescription ever given for maintaining a spiritual well-being as chronic medication. Pray 3 times a day before meals. Philippians 2:3,4, says, "Do nothing from selfish or empty conceit, but with humility of mind regard one another as more important than yourselves; do not merely look out for your own personal interests, but also for the interests of others."

It is the best gift given to any person in need, physically, emotionally, financially, materially, relationally and spiritually. What is humanly impossible is possible with

God, who can flatten every mountain that stands before us, and who can straighten every crooked path before us, who can create rivers in the desert. He will walk with us through the waters without us drowning, and He will go with us through the fire without us being consumed. He will always take our weak hands in His big strong hands to hold, lead and guide us into the paths of righteousness. We do not have answers to all the questions, but prayer is the solution.   It is the resolution, the path to finding answers to problems. It provides insight for our dilemmas and tough decisions. God says, **"Ask me and I will tell you remarkable secrets you do not know about things to come," Jeremiah 33:3.**

Prayer is making supplication and intercession for those we care about. Interceding is reaching to meet people, to make urgent petitions on their behalf, when they are experiencing challenges. We reach God, meet God and entreat Him for His favour. He promises to hear and answer and show us great and mighty things, more that we can ever hope to imagine.

Luke 11:9,10, promises, **"So I tell you, keep on asking, and you will receive what you ask for. Keep on seeking, and you will find. Keep on knocking and the door will be opened to you. For everyone who asks, receives. Everyone who seeks finds, and everyone who knocks, the door will be opened."** With assurances as such, we would all become converted to receive from the hand of God Almighty.

Through our intercession people's lives will be spared. We should never underestimate the possibility of a reversal of God's judgment through our loving prayers. When friends, family and leaders are in a crisis, we should prepare to pay the price in intercession. We can pray for the impossible and never limit God's ability. **2 Chronicles 7:14,** reminds us, **"If My people who are called by My name will humble themselves and pray and seek My face and turn from their wicked ways, I WILL hear from heaven, forgive their sins and restore their land. My eyes will be open and My ears will be attentive to every prayer."**

During dry times our provision of kindness will take the form of praise and worship. Praising God will be like water flowing from a well. It will be refreshing, cleansing and causing growth. When we gather people together, there will be unity and power in corporate gatherings. When there is unanimous praise, God demonstrates His power. He promises to give us water, life giving water; when we are responsible. Our lesson learned will be to sing in times of depression, anxiety or pressure. Taking people away when they are in the doldrums, will lift up their spirits and add joy to their downtrodden spirits.

They will not become self- reliant, but God-dependent. Their plans will not take priority, they will not conform to the world's dictates and standards, but will see the power and might of God's hands over their lives. What the enemy has used as evil and a weakness, God will convert to strength and goodness to promote His kingdom. Our greatest sacrifice and act of submission is laying down our agenda and picking up Christ's to expand God's territory and bring about salvation. We can emulate our Lord. He said, "Father, if you are willing, please take this cup of suffering away from me. Yet I want your will to be done, not mine," Luke 22:42. We have to turn from our selfish ways, take up our cross and follow Him.

Praying for others to become wiser, will help them make well thought out decisions, not rash ones which will have negative effects. They can be taught to ask. God says, "If you need wisdom, ask our generous God, and He will give it to you," James 1:5. Our constant prayer can be asking God to grant spiritual wisdom and insight to grow in His knowledge.

Prayer is necessary to know more:

- The more they know, the better prepared they will be.
- The more they know, the more equipped they will be to make decisions.
- The more they know, the more qualified they are to explain.
- The more they know, the better they can connect.
- The more they know, the better they will discern.
- The more they know, the more adept they will be for endorsing the good news.

It will broaden their concepts about spiritual living and total dependence on their Creator.

BENEFITS OF PRAYING WITH PEOPLE

Lonely, troubled, fearful people do not want to be alone, but are afraid to request for companionship; and instead wallow in self-pity. Identifying them and making time to visit and pray with them would be a great encouragement and edification. **Ecclesiastes 4:9-10**, reassures us that,

"Two people are better than one or they can help each other succeed. If one person falls, the other can reach out and help."

Praying with people allows them to share their burdens with us, making it lighter. A burden shared is a burden halved. We are made transparent and vulnerable too, when we reveal how we overcame our struggles. This revelation of ourselves strengthens trust builds relationships and inspires them to know that they are not alone. "We obey the law of Christ when we share each other's burdens," Galatians 6:2.

In **Matthew 18:19**, we are assured that **if two shall agree on earth as touching anything that they shall ask, it shall be done for them.** It removes room for doubt and wavering, and strengthens their belief and faith. Listening to other people pray with them will remove every hindrance and grant them hope. Praying with others is mutually beneficial, both partners will be blessed. It allows us to do an introspection and look at our own needs, enabling us to squelch any form of selfishness and minimize our own challenges. Corporate prayer develops concern for others, demonstrating the fruit of the Spirit of kindness. Let us make this world a better place, by putting others first.

By praying with others we avert them from the temptation to sin, and not yield to suicidal thoughts. We can pray for help to keep them from making wrong choices, and to give them the strength to do what is right. The Holy Spirit is invited into their lives, to comfort, direct and provide answers.

Prayer is how we reach out to God; and let Him reach into our hearts to fill us with His love. It blesses us and the people who we pray for and brings peace into their hearts and homes. Prayers are answered in the form of thoughts, spiritual feelings, scriptures, voices and actions of other people. As prayer partners, we are able to mentor the needy, weak-willed, frail and spiritually sick to experience personal miracles, such as peace, healing and forgiveness of sins.

CS Lewis is often attributed as saying, "Prayer doesn't change God, it changes me."

We need to teach others to learn to put God first, and not to lean on our own understanding. Stress is a silent killer, let us eradicate it with prayer. It is our only line of defence against every attack of the enemy. In Philippians 4:6, we are told to, "be anxious for nothing, but in everything by prayer and supplication, with thanksgiving, let your requests be made known to God."

Prayer is preventative instead of being a remedy, so let us call upon our Lord first and not as a last resort. Let us become dependent on God and not on man. If prayer becomes our lifestyle, then everything that happens in our lives will be the result of God's superintendence. We must remember that when we turn our eyes away from our inadequacies, we turn to God's sufficiency.

Prayer is aligning ourselves with
the purposes of God.

– E. Stanley Jones

Paradoxical Commandments

CHAPTER 22

People are illogical, unreasonable, and self-centred.
Love them anyway.

If you do good, people will accuse you of selfish ulterior
motives.
Do good anyway.

If you are successful, you will win false friends and true
enemies.
Succeed anyway.

The good you do today will be forgotten tomorrow.
Do good anyway.

Honesty and frankness make you vulnerable.
Be honest and frank anyway.

The biggest men and women with the biggest ideas can
be shot down by the smallest men and women with the
smallest minds.
Think big anyway.

People favour underdogs but follow only top dogs.
Fight for a few underdogs anyway.

What you spend years building may be destroyed
overnight.
Build anyway.

People really need help but may attack you if you do
help them.
Help people anyway.

Give the world the best you have and you'll get kicked
in the teeth.
Give the world the best you have anyway."

– Kent M. Keith

"A random act of kindness, no matter how small, can
make a tremendous impact on someone else's life."
– Roy T. Bennett

ACTS OF KINDNESS

CHAPTER 23

ACTS OF KINDNESS FOR KIDS TOWARDS PARENTS

- Surprise Mom by making the bed.
- Help set the table before meals.
- Help tidy up after meals.
- Clean mum's or dad's car.
- Make Mom breakfast.
- Bring Mum a flower.
- Help hang or fold the washing.
- Play with your brother or sister.

- Babysit siblings so mum can take a nap.
- Be a great version of yourself.
- Do not throw tantrums.
- Listen to instructions and act on them.
- Feed the pets.
- Walk the dog.
- Clean the pet's habitat.
- Pick up the dog's pooh.
- Mow the lawn if you can.
- Help to pack away the groceries.
- Eat the lunch that was packed for you.
- Do chores without being asked.

ACTS OF KINDNESS AT SCHOOL

- Make a card for someone who is ill.
- Share with someone who does not have.
- Include everyone in activities at school.
- Help at homework time.
- Invite someone for a play date.
- Put a nice note on your teacher's desk.
- Put a nice note on someone's desk.
- Pick something up for someone.
- Stand up to a bully.
- Admit when you're wrong and say sorry.

- Don't talk behind someone's back.
- Don't be a talebearer.
- Make someone a birthday card.
- Treat everyone with respect.
- Help your teacher by carrying her bag.
- Do your best at school.
- Be the new kid's friend.
- Help tidy your classroom.
- Run an errand for your teacher.
- Let others have your turn.
- Ask before you use someone's stuff.
- Pay attention!

ACTS OF KINDNESS TO STRANGERS.

- Greet everyone you see.
- Smile, it beautifies your face.
- Carry an elderly person's shopping bag.
- Open the door for a disabled person.
- Put a smile on the face of a sad person.
- Give gifts at your birthday party.
- Let an elderly person sit while you stand.
- Return shopping trolleys.
- Pick up rubbish.
- Throw trash into a bin.
- Talk to the lonely.

- Give a flower to an old lady.
- Mow your neighbour's lawn, if you can.
- Compliment someone daily.
- Surprise someone with a gift.
- Pick up fallen garments in a store.
- Share your umbrella on a rainy day.
- Make little gifts for the needy.
- Make cheer up cards.
- Do a job without expecting any payment.
- Help out when someone is sick.
- Donate unwanted toys and games.
- Put flowers on cars in the carpark.
- Leave a treat for the cashier.
- Be grateful for what you receive.
- Forgive someone who hurt you.
- Use your manners.
- Ask for donations for a charity.
- Be kind to the blind, deaf and mute.

ACTS OF KINDNESS FOR ADULTS AT HOME

- Adopt a pet from an animal shelter.
- Ask for donations for a charity.
- Spend time on the floor to see the world from a child's perspective.
- Do not yell at each other.

- Treat everyone with respect and dignity.
- Treat everyone the same, do not have favourites.
- Help mum or dad with chores.
- Don't sit around, while everyone else is busy, lend a helping hand.
- When the helper is away, help with the chores.
- Help with the children, it isn't only mum's job.
- Help with the pets.
- Bath the dogs.
- Pick up the pooh.
- Mow the lawn.
- Clean the pool.
- Tidy up after the kids have messed.
- Prepare meals occasionally.
- Hang the washing.
- Pack the washing away.
- Help with the ironing.
- Give a good foot massage at the end of a tiring day.
- Share the television remote.
- Do not hog the television.
- Treat everyone as you would like to be treated.

ACTS OF KINDNESS AT WORK

- Greet everyone with a cheery 'Good Morning'
- Make time to have a quick chat with colleagues.

- Remember your Boss's birthday.
- Help where you can, without being asked.
- Treat everyone with dignity.
- Be ever ready to lend a helping hand.
- Do not be a snitch.
- Be a shoulder for others to lean or cry on.
- Look out for others, not yourself.
- Tell your bosses they're doing a good job.
- Compliment co workers.
- Share your umbrella on a rainy day.
- Don't participate in gossip.
- Leave a positive note on a work colleague's desk.
- Give your seat to someone who needs it more.
- Invite a colleague for coffee.
- Be a listening ear.
- Appreciate people's efforts without criticising.
- Accept criticism, without throwing a fit.
- Don't say negative things.
- Pick up the downtrodden.
- Create a book of memories.
- Encourage people to follow their dreams.
- Encourage colleagues to do their best, especially when no one is watching.
- Make the workplace a pleasant place, you spend most of your time there.

ACTS OF KINDNESS TO STRANGERS

- Buy coffee for the person behind you.
- Wave at children in cars
- Help elderly people put groceries in their car and return their trolley.
- Mow your neighbours' outside lawn when mowing your lawn.
- Share unwanted books with friends.
- Call or send a card to let someone know that you're thinking of them.
- Put a rand or positive note in a library book before you return it.
- Drop some coins where children can easily find them.
- Contribute to a child's school lunch account.
- Put change in vending machines.
- Keep an eye on your neighbour's home while they're away.
- Leave bubble mixture in a park for children to find.
- Buy a movie ticket for the person behind you.
- Offer to take a group photo so everyone can be in the picture.
- Convert loyalty points to gift cards and give to someone in need.
- Volunteer at a non-profit organisation.
- Take someone out who doesn't drive.
- Take unwanted toys or games to a children's hospital.
- Compliment someone with a lovely garden with a

    note in their letterbox.

- Bake a cake for a needy family.
- Pay a compliment.
- Make extras to share when you're cooking, baking, and preserving.
- Share produce from your garden.
- Give someone a ride to town.
- Send a small gift and a kindness card through
- Participate in community - upliftment programmes.
- Make care bags for the homeless.
- Mentor the kids in your neighbourhood.
- When someone wants to repay you for something, ask them to do something good for others instead, "Pay it forward."

Acts of kindness will warm cold hearts, bring a smile to the lips and maybe a tear of joy to the eyes.

– Rose Reddy

PAY IT FORWARD

CHAPTER 24

Respond to someone's kindness to you by being kind to someone else.

The simplest way to define **"pay it forward"** is when someone does something for you, instead of paying that person back directly, you pass it on to another person instead. A good example to note is if someone buys you a cup of coffee you should buy the person behind you a cup of coffee. This concept dates back to 317 BC, where it was used as a key plot in a play, "*The Grouch*" in ancient Athens. It became very popular after the movie "Pay it Forward" in the year 2000.

What happens when you pay it forward? We ask people to repay our kindness by doing a good deed for someone else. The purpose of the 'pay it forward' principle is to build kindness exponentially in the community, and to remind people that one good deed deserves another.

It makes the world a better place and can become a part of our daily lives. It will enhance our personal and professional lives. We will be taught life's lessons in compassion and service, by teaching us that we shouldn't be narcissistic, entitled and shouldn't expect instant gratification.

We should perform good deeds for no particular reason and with no expected return. This act can be performed on people who we don't even know. We should be encouraged to be kind without selfish motivations. Only after performing acts of kindness, will we realize how rewarding it is to be kind. People will show their appreciation by returning the favour and doing something nice for us; instead they should be encouraged to do it for someone else, and keep spreading kindness to more people. An excellent way to create awareness, is to ask people who want to reciprocate your act of kindness to instead do something nice to three other people.

If that action is repeated, then your one good deed will quickly be changed into thirteen good deeds. A little act of kindness can go a long way and even become contagious. Selfishness is a response to pain, and if it continues, it becomes the greatest cause of misery; instead let us introduce kindness as the antidote for pain. Selfishness will then be converted to selflessness. Any act of kindness, regardless of the size will make a difference; especially when done intentionally. Dalai Lama, is quoted, "Kindness is my religion." If we all adopt that philosophy, and let kindness go viral; then this world would be a better place. This revolution can begin with us, if each one of us intentionally performed an act of kindness. One simple act will reveal a genuine generosity of spirit and put smiles on downcast faces and brighten their days. This will attract others to the cause and multiply itself into countless acts of kindness. Our creativity, spontaneity and charity will inspire others to create a kinder and prudent world. The unconditional benevolence and munificence will deliver unadulterated compassion to follow in like manner, continuing the cycle of kindness. When an act of kindness is experienced, it leaves a warm feeling of love and acceptance. When acts of kindness are performed, a note could accompany it; stating, "You have just been touched by an act of kindness. Be inspired and use this note to perform acts of kindness to someone else. Pay it forward."

"If you can't pay it back, pay it forward."
– Catherine Ryan Hyde

WISE WORDS TO LIVE BY

CHAPTER 25

L et all bitterness, wrath, anger, clamour and evil speaking be put away from you, with all malice. And be kind to one another, tender-hearted, forgiving one another.
Ephesians 4:31, 32

He is kind to the ungrateful and wicked.
Luke 6:35

This kindness is greater than that which you showed earlier.
Ruth 3:10.

Blessed is he of the Lord, who hath not left off his
kindness to the living and the dead.
Ruth 2:20

The islanders showed us unusual kindness. They built a
fire and welcomed us all because it was raining and
cold.
Acts 28:2

The kindness and love of God our Saviour saved us,
because of his mercy.
Titus 3:4

Love must be sincere. Hate what is evil; cling to what is
good.
Romans 12:9

If it is in serving, then serve; if it is in teaching, then
teach; if it is to encourage, then give encouragement; if
it is giving, then give generously; if it is to lead, do it
diligently; if it is to show mercy, do it cheerfully.
Romans 12:7

Be kindly affectionate to one another with brotherly
love, in honour giving preference to one another; not
lagging in diligence, fervent in spirit, serving the Lord;
rejoicing in hope, patient in tribulation, continuing
steadfastly in prayer, distributing to the needs of the
saints, given to hospitality.
Romans 12:10 -13

Bless those who persecute you, bless and do not curse.
Romans 12:14

Rejoice with those who rejoice, and weep with those who weep.
Romans 12:15

Live in harmony with one another.
Romans 12:16

Do not be proud, but be willing to associate with people of low position.
Romans 12:16

Do not be conceited.
Romans 12:16

Do not repay anyone evil for evil.
Romans 12:17

Be careful to do what is right in the eyes of everyone.
Romans 12:17

Live at peace with everyone.
Romans 12:18

Do not take revenge.
Romans 12:19

If your enemy is hungry, feed him; if he is thirsty, give
him something to drink.
Romans 7:20

Do not be overcome by evil, but overcome evil with
good. Romans 12: 7-21.

Hear me, O Lord; for thy lovingkindness is good.
Psalm 69:16

Love suffers long and is kind.
1 Corinthians 13:4

She opens her mouth with wisdom, and the teaching of
kindness is on her tongue.
Proverbs 31:26

Put on then, as God's chosen ones, holy and beloved,
compassionate hearts, kindness, humility, meekness
and patience, bearing with one another and, if one has a
complaint against another, forgiving each other; as the
Lord has forgiven you, so you must also forgive.
Colossians 3:12

But the fruit of the Spirit is love, joy, peace, patience,
kindness, goodness, faithfulness and gentleness.
Galatians 5: 22, 23

Don't be afraid, for I will surely show you kindness for
the sake of your father Jonathan, I will restore to you all
the land that belonged to your grandfather Saul, and
you will always eat at my table.
2 Samuel 9:7

Show me unfailing kindness like the Lord's kindness as
long as I live, so that I may not be killed.
1 Samuel 20:14

I will show kindness because his father showed kindness to me.
1 Chronicles 19:2

Whoever pursues righteousness and kindness will find
life, righteousness and honour.
Proverbs 21:21

- A man who is kind benefits himself, but a cruel man
hurts himself.
Proverbs 11:17

Note then the kindness and severity of God: severity
towards those who have fallen, but God's kindness to
you, provided you continue in His kindness.
Romans 11:22

Feed the hungry, quench the thirst, invite strangers in,
clothe the naked, look after the sick, visit the prisoner.
Matthew 25:35,36

Do all things without murmurings and disputings?
Philippians 2:14
Whosoever compels you to go a mile, go with him two.
Matthew 5:41

Give to those who ask, to borrow; do not turn them
away.
Matthew 5:42

Withhold not good from them to whom it is due, when
it is in the power of your hand to do it.
Proverbs 3:27

The Lord says, "I will guide you along the best pathway
for your life. I will advise you and watch over you."
Psalm 32:8

*We are dedicated to bringing humanity back to it God's
given purpose of living a fulfilled, accepted, life of
civility.*
– Rose Reddy

THE  KINDNESS FOUNDATION

CONCLUSION

The Searcher, within me has been obedient to the voice of God, which was impressed upon my heart to pen Kindness, a Building Block of Civility, because humanity has removed itself from all forms of dignity by professing to be wise, darkening their foolish hearts and becoming futile in their thoughts.

Let us forget the past and reach for those things that still lay ahead, that we may walk worthy of our calling to the Lord and please Him. As we grow in His knowledge we can become more fruitful, to help man throw off the old self and lifestyle that depicts the worldly systems and put on the new which is created in Christ's image. Let us put on love, be tender, merciful, humble, patient, forgiving and kind.

This is part of the I Change Nations initiative to bring change, one step at a time; by diligently seeking unity in our thoughts, attitudes, love, spirit and purpose. We have to humble ourselves in service to each other, making nobodies feel like somebodies. This can be done by spreading **K**nowledge, which **I**ntroduces **N**otions and **D**esigns **N**ecessary for **E**ssential **S**uccessful **S**tewardship. **KINDNESS**

When that is done then **K**ingdom **I**ntegrated **N**ations will be **D**eveloped through **N**otions that are **E**ssential for **S**pirited **S**aturated citizens. **KINDNESS**

I am part of the I CHANGE NATIONS group of people who have their ears attached to the mouth of God, waiting to hear Him speak and to act upon it. This is an awesome, innovative, productive and professional group who are changing the world. Their influence is not numerical, but exponential. His Majesty, Sir Clyde Rivers, heads the flagship with Professor Michal Pitzl. They have been instrumental in creating the UGSCI Programmes. Professor Michal Pitzl has coined new terminology ' *Searcherdemics, Searcherdemicians.*' It is a philosophy that she has studied and researched. It is a brand new form of education called Life Education. It is God's Education System which is inclusive, whereby the Holy Spirit is the teacher. This narrative causes people to believe in themselves and their God ideas and expose it to the world bringing validation and transformation.

This is the team of dedicated professors who are working together at United Graduate College and Seminary International:

1. Professors Chris and Carol Green, founders of the C.A.R.E. Program are our Chancellors.

2. Professor Mateus Mutola, is the youngest Professor in Mozambique and is our Vice Chancellor and promoter of Geniusology.

3. Professor Glendon Rudder from Trinidad and Tobago -Founder, Pan-Evangelism & Pan-Evangelistic World Outreach, Founder and Lecturer, Human Equity Value

4. Alicia Kipps Rudder of Trinidad and Tobago - Psychopnumology.

5. Professor Phinehas Kunithia – Dream Actualisation Expert.

6. Professor Gillian Businga – London Founder of Royal Civility Global Initiative

7. Professor Patrick Businga- London Greatness University

8. Professor Vernet Alin Joseph from America – Potential, Passion & Productivity Speaker, Strategist & Consultant.

9. Professor Jared Akama Onyari- Kenya Chancellor Liaison

10. Dr. Linda Lara- America, Founder, Future Elite Academy, Recognized Master Civility Trainer, an

Entrepreneur, Award Winning Community Change Maker

11. Professor Christine Kozachuk – USA, Founder, Every Girl Wins Institute, Founder, Her Right Initiative, International World Civility Ambassador.

It is a great honour to be associated with such an awesome group of people who are changing the world and making it a better place every day. Let us live by the Golden Rule: "Do unto others as you would have them do unto you." Whether it is inscribed on the pages of the Holy Bible or any other religious material, let us apply it to our everyday activity. It is simple but effective to bring humanity back to humanity. Let it govern our hearts and become the hallmark of our strong and healthy moral system. When we have the ability to understand and share the feelings of others we will guard our speech and actions, become empathetic in impacting our world positively.

We are the light of the world. Let our light shine before others, that they may see our good deeds and glorify our Father in heaven.

Matthew 5:14, 16

BIBLIOGRAPHY

1. Anyway Paradoxical Commandments
    https://www.paradoxicalcommandments.com/
2. Charles Darwin
    https://www.khanacademy.org/science/ap-biology/naturalevolution-natural-
3. Dr. Benjamin Spock
    https://simple.wikipedia.org/wiki/Benjamin_Spoc
    k
4. Friedrich Nietzsche's Moral and Political Philosophy
    https://plato.stanford.edu/entries/nietzsche-moral-political/

5. Holy Bible
    https://www.google.com/search?q=biblegateway
6. Importance of Prayer
    https://www.prayerandpossibilities.com/importa
    nce-daily-prayer/.
7. Kindness in South Africa
    https://www.sangofrontline.co.za/top-10-ngos-in-
    south-africa/
8. Mohandas Karamchand Gandhi
    https://en.wikipedia.org/wiki/Mahatma_Gandhi
9. Oprah Winfrey
    https://en.wikipedia.org/wiki/Oprah_Winfrey
10. Paying it Forward
    https://www.bryantstratton.edu/blog/what-does-
    it-mean-to-pay-it-forward#
11. Sigmund Freud
    https://en.wikipedia.org/wiki/Sigmund_Freud
12. What is education?
    https://en.wikipedia.org/wiki/Education
13. What is Forgiveness and its Benefits
    https://positivepsychology.com/forgiveness-
    benefits/
14. What is kindness?
    https://en.wikipedia.org/wiki/Kindness

ABOUT THE AUTHOR

Prof. Shakuntala Reddy, (Rose) is a powerful international -inspirational speaker, Professor at United Graduate College and Seminary International- USA, industry
leader, author, faith-based and Christian counsellor. The
African Civility Educator of the year 2021 - I Change
Nations. She has trained & certified 35 students in Biblical
counselling. Her thesis is entitled "The Ripple Effects of
Multiple Parenting".

Founder of The Rose Kindness Foundation, a non profit organization – Sanctuary for abused women and children, unwed mothers, the homeless, drug & alcohol addicts. She's presently the Departmental Head of the Foundation Phase at Richards Bay Primary School, South Africa. As a global kindness and civility trainer for more than three decades, Prof. Reddy's success is based on her ability to assist organizations and individuals achieve real results. Her experiences as a professional educator, corporate and executive coach, mentor, enterprising businesswoman, and strategic consultant allow her to share her proven strategies for building civility value, inspiring innovation, and generating sustainable growth.

She offers an internship focusing on civility and kindness, training and certification in biblical counselling and sustainable development that utilizes the talents, skills, and passions of all involved to build a more conscious world.

She acquired diplomas in the following:

Pre -Junior Primary Education: Springfield College of Education

Higher Education Diploma in Remedial Education: Springfield College of Education

Educational Management: MANCOSA

Theology: Teamwork Bible College of South Africa

Advanced Christian Counselling – with a practice number to Counsel: Faith Bible College Johannesburg

She acquired degrees in the following:
Bachelor in Christian Counselling UGCSI California, USA
Masters in Christian Counselling UGCSI California, USA
Doctorate in Christian Counselling: UGCSI California, USA
Dissertation Title: "The Ripple effect of Multiple Parenting"
 Doctorate in Searcherdemics – God's Education System: UGCSI California, USA

Appointments:
Principal: New Life Ministries Bible College
Member of the Academic Council: UGCSI
Online International Professor: UGCSI

Work Experience:
Foundation Phase Educator
School Counsellor/Mentor
Prayer Group Leader
Head of Department Foundation Phase: Richards Bay Primary School

Clergy Jobs:
Children's Church Teacher & Superintendent
Women's Group Leader
Bible Study Teacher
Intercession Leader
Preacher
Biblical Counsellor

Pioneer & Overseer of Private School: New Life Academy
Active Member: INKOSI Community Projects

Annual Youth Day Events:
Float processions, fun & games, motivational speakers
Preparing of banners, feeding schemes, sporting events,
sponsorships/fund raising drives